Shades of Ritual

Minority Voices in Practice

Contributing Authors Include

Nadirah Adeye
Clio Ajana
Crystal Blanton
Flame Bridhesdottir
Leslie Brooks
Janet Callahan
Alexandra Chauran
Dr. Katharyn Privett-Duren (Seba O'Kiley)
Yutaka Furuki
Abel R. Gomez
Olivia Haynes
Yvonne E. Nieves
Luna Pantera
Nathaniel Puckett
Rt. Rev. Anniitra Ravenmoon
Sandra Santiago
Szmeralda Shanel
Rose Skye
Jayde Van Ter Pool
Pablo Vazquez III
Heaven Walker
Cecily Joy Willowe, M.Div.
Alisa Kuumba Zuwena

Shades of Ritual
Minority Voices in Practice

Edited by Crystal Blanton

Megalithica Books
Stafford England

Shades of Ritual: Minority Voices in Practice
Edited by Crystal Blanton
© 2014 First edition

All rights reserved, including the right to reproduce this book, or portions thereof, in any form.

The rights of the individual contributors to be identified as the authors of this work have been asserted by them in accordance with the Copyright, Designs and Patents Act, 1988.

Editor: Crystal Blanton
Layout: Taylor Ellwood
Cover Design: Storm Constantine
Cover Photograph: Shu Yamaguchi
Cover Photo model: Luna Pantera

Set in Book Antiqua

MB0170

ISBN 978-1-905713-96-7

A Megalithica Books Publication
An imprint of Immanion Press

info@immanion-press.com
http://www.immanion-press.com

Dedication

I would like specifically honor one of the authors within this anthology who recently crossed over to the land of the ancestors, Alisa Kuumba Zuwena. She was very excited about the production of this anthology and being a part of its manifestation. Kuumba died on April 22, 2014, before being able to see the very book she was able to be a part of creating. We are honored to have her words, and her voice, as a part of this anthology, and want to honor her spirit in the final production and distribution of this incredible collection of work. What a beautiful gift she left for us all to share, and for that we are all grateful.

Contents

Introduction	7
Black Wicca: On Becoming a Womanist Wiccan	9
Loving My Blackness: A Personal Reflection	19
The Many Faces of Athena	22
The Other Southerner	34
The Magic of Memory; Authentic Ancestral Exchange	40
This Land Is Your Land	45
My Blood Song	47
Acts of Love and Pleasure: Self Nurture as a Revolutionary Art or An Introduction to the Art of Sacred Sensuality	58
Paganism and the Path Back to Africa	71
On Those Whose Shoulders We Stand	75
Finding Divinity in the Deep South	81
Stereotypes, Prejudice, and the Impact on Spiritual or Magical Workings	88
The Voice of the Ancestors	100
Starting Small	108
Do You Even Know Me?	111
A Candle for Remembrance; A Juneteenth Working	117
Who Are You and What Do You Do	119
Foxtrot in Flames	126
Honoring Ancestors When You Don't Know Who They Are	127
Multicultural Paganism – How to Find Your Way	131
Conjuring Woman	136
Pagan Nepantla: Searching for Identity	138
The Smudge Stick	143
Circle of Understanding	147
Finding Your Place: My Socio-Emotional-Political Practice	151
Delphian Whispers	159
My Love of Serpents	159
Quinquatrus	162
West in East	167
The Long Quest for the Goddess	176
Biographies	182

Introduction

The combination of cultures can bring about such wealth and beauty in practice, yet it can also be a part of a complex, and often complicated journey to spiritual practice. The path to uncovering an authentic spiritual practice is not necessarily an easy one for anyone, a multitude of elements added onto this can make it that much more lively.

The unfolding project that became *Shade of Faith; Minority Voices in Paganism*, opened up an avenue of discussions about the incredible journeys of people of color within the Pagan path. It also brought about an increased desire to continue the platform of writing for People of color that are practitioners, and how practicing a Pagan path is influenced by ethnic culture.

As the world within Paganism adjusts to the many different faces around the circle, we are all adjusting to the dance of community that is so diverse and varied in their presentation, beliefs and practitioners. We are the mixture of brown-faced reflections of our ancestors, stepping out of the shadows of the overculture, and becoming a part of the visible diversity of our community. The color of my pigmented skin does not separate me from community, but the various cultural nuances of my practice is not always accepted within the collective worship circle. While some practices are ancient, some are new, wrapped up in a lineage that solidifies our place within the circle.

The stories of these practitioners show a resilience that becomes the foundation for spiritual practice, the motivation for academic research, and the spirit behind breaking down compartmentalized sections of our lives between the box that contains ethnicity and the box that contains our spirituality. It is all of those things, and none of those things that make up the Pagans of color experience within this community, and within their own homes.

This unfolding project became Shades of Ritual; Minority Voices in Practice, the product of many discussions, much to share, and a desire to show another layer of the unfolding diversity within our vast community of magical practitioners.

The thoughts, reflections, practices, rituals, and writings contained within this book are from the author's themselves, in their own voice, and with their own flavor. All different, a myriad of differences, these pieces show the similarities and complexities of vastly different practices and cultures. Together we present these pieces to you.

May you enjoy them in the spirit they were written, with love, complexity, beauty, power, magic, and sincerity.

Crystal Blanton
2014

Black Wicca:
On Becoming a Womanist Wiccan

Cecily Joy Willowe, M.Div

I grew up in many churches. I was dragged to whatever church the family member who was babysitting me belonged to. I remember Baptist, Lutheran and Black Catholic churches. Growing up they all were the same to me, some had communion with wafers and others didn't. But they all were long, loud, mostly entertaining, and always a bit strange: big hats, praising Jesus and getting the Holy Spirit. However, my official church was a Methodist church in Chicago, where my mother and I were one of the first Black members. I do not remember that ever being a problem. I actually don't remember much about that church except going to Sunday school, having picture day and the music. I remember we sang and clapped a lot. I remember that "He's Got the Whole World in His Hands" seemed to be the church's theme song. Then in my pre-teens we moved to the suburbs and for the rest of my young adult life, I was without a church. I was no longer going to my own or visiting varieties around Chicago.

I grew up without a theology placed upon me. I recalled songs and clapping of White people, and dancing, praising and the falling over of Black people. I recalled the sounds, movements and rituals of church. But I never got much meaning out of it. The little Christian theology that I was taught never sat right with me. I had more questions than revelations. For example, I was constantly asked "How could Cain marry someone outside his family when it says his family was the only one". But no matter how many times I asked my questions, I never got satisfying answers. Even as a child, I could not go on faith alone.

Now, in my teen years, there were no churches, no questions to rise to an empty crowd. We lived for many years without a spirit center. Yet, the spirit did not leave me. I started to talk to Jesus in my head and ponder religion questions to myself until I found New Age philosophy and I abandoned Christ for more exciting things like tarot cards and spirit guides. Tarot card reading and spirit guide communication became my practice. It was a way of knowing that I was not alone in world, that I was part of something greater and mysterious. It was my first bit of evidence that there were spirits around us, guiding us and loving us. I prefer them to a God and Son who felt too judgmental for me. I wanted a Divine voice that said Hindus to Christians were all equal. For a long time, that religious neutrality and spiritual open-minded state was enough. Until, I entered my own journey into the darkness of the soul.

It was in an English composition, listening to a young girl's paper on Witches, where I first learned about Wicca. I was caught by the religion where magic was possible, where love for nature was the center and the result was a radical acceptance of an earthly and spiritual life. I did not begin my quest to learn more about this quirky religion until later during the winter holiday season. I had just broke up with my fiancée' and was deep into a battle with depression. I was out of school and had no job. My idle hands were slowly driving me crazy. I do not know why it was then that I decided to research this religion that piqued my interest. I suppose the spirits were guiding me, telling me I needed something more now than a deck of divination cards. I needed something that would ground me, excite me and gave me a new faith in life. Wicca did just that. Wiccan practice from nature celebrations, rituals, spells and energy work gave me my first taste of being infinite. The rituals taught me that I could communicate with nature, have my will and be guided by nature's grace. It gave me control of my life, reality and body. After years fighting anxiety and depression, Wicca was my avenue to peace of mind and body.

For a long time, the bliss that Wiccan practice gave me, shielded me from the fact that Wicca was not based in my cultural understanding. The only thing Black about Wicca was a few darker aspects of the Goddess. The mythology, rituals and most of the practitioners were loaded in Eurocentrism. The whiteness of Wicca did not hit me until I moved from my predominately Black suburb to the extremely White, Boulder, Colorado, for graduate school.

The cultural shock was not instant. It was a slow draining realization that I could go a week without seeing another Black person. I could go months without having a solid conversation with someone from my culture. I become angry and traumatized by all the subtle racism that I faced. The Tibetan Buddhism I was studying, in my Master of Divinity program, held no relief from that isolation and trauma. Many of the students were happy to just meditate instead of doing any spiritual or social action. Yet, all the meditation in the world could not make racism disappear and make Black people materialize in Colorado. In the silence of Buddhist meditation, I began to miss the loudness and heat of Black reverence and social action.

It was an assignment in an interreligious dialogue class that led to the next step in my spiritual practice. For a project we were asked to research and portray an historical or modern theologian. I decided to play the role of Alice Walker; the writer, social activist and Womanist. It was in her Womanist prose that I finally found a kindred spirit and elder. Her life story modeled exactly what I hoped to one day achieve: activism that focused on insectionality, on the healing of oppressed people and the realization that all life is interconnected. In Walker's definition of Womanism, I found the description of my own inner spirit. A Womanist, as she put it, is someone who, "Loves music. Loves dance. Loves the moon. Loves the Spirit. Loves love and food and roundness. Loves struggle. Loves the Folk. Loves herself. Regardless. (Walker, 2005)" For the first time in long time, I saw myself fully in someone's description of the Divine. The spirit was not a White jealous God or a White motherly figure. The spirit was the radical, full and loving Black woman.

After finally seeing myself within a theological landscape, I took to learning more about Womanist theology. Womanist theology is a liberation and social justice perspective based off the writings of Alice Walker, liberation theology, feminist theology and Black liberation theology. Womanist theology analyzes theology, and creates practices based on experiences of Black women and other oppressed people. It focuses on the intersection of race, gender, class and various marginalizations. Although, Walker is a self-acclaimed Pagan and also partial to Buddhism, Womanist theology has for the most part been applied to Christianity and the culture of Black church. I decided to bring the Womanist back into Paganism, and developed a Womanist approach to my Wiccan practice.

What I realized from combining Wiccan and Womanist theology was that Wicca could be more than spells, bells and shiny things. It was helping me work through various forms of trauma, healing me in ways I could not describe or know until Womanism gave me the words. I was coming into a practice that was healing the wound of feeling lost. I felt, like many Black Americans, that I had no place on this earth to call my own. I was not seen as African or American. Wicca showed me that I did not need a place on a map to call my origins. It would be nice, but I belong to nature, the earth, the Goddess. Wicca made the ground, the skies, the stars, and the universe my home. Everything was my place and I was a place for everything. It became ok to be lost, lost in the vastness of myself, my being, of home. Home had no beginning or end. Home became a lovely mystery and adventure instead of a throbbing wound.

This kind of cultural healing is an important part of my Wiccan Womanist spiritual practice. Getting through the past injustices and surviving the currents ones are the essential of my practice. Black people are suffering so much. Black spirituality has to be political in order to survive. I was once asked if I could have a spiritual practice separate from social activism. I laughed and replied, "I'm Black." Then I added, "Every day I live. That is a radical act." There is so much going against Black people today. We deal with the subtle and obvious racism which raises our blood pressure, causes mental illness and lowers our life expectancy. The racist world out there is trying to kill us. Often it succeeds, with gunshots or slow death of degradation. It is even a miracle for a Black child to be born, with high infant mortality rates. To live a long life as a Black person is a radical act. To be happy is even more so.

Yes, spiritual healing is political. In church we talk about God helping us through the racist world. We ask God for help finding good homes, employment. But we also asked that he help with civil issues. Civil action is the reality of a Black life. Black American spirituality has always included it. Black spirituality has always been about healing cultural wounds. It reminds us of our dignity, our connectedness to our bodies, families and community. All of which was stolen from us when our bodies became commodities. Spiritual practice is a place to remember our lost cultures and practices. Black people add these practices to the bible so they could not be taken away no matter how hard the White master tried. In my spiritual practice I do the same. I put my Black practices, ideas and beliefs into Wicca. At first, I did not even realize that I could approach Wicca from my place of blackness. Then through a Womanist approach, I started adding my culture to my practices more purposely. I started to add rituals for culture healing, social justice, dealing with trauma and various political based rites. I decided that my practice would include all my life, all my pains, all victories and all my history. After all, one does not stop being Black the moment they pick up a wand.

Now, as a self-proclaimed, Womanist Wiccan, I have become disenchanted with the Whiteness of the common Wiccan Gods. I need images of the Divine that look like me. I needed to commune with Spirits that understand a Black Women's spiritual needs and purpose. With this new drive to find myself in the face of the Gods and to meet my ancestors, I took to studying Orishas and Voodoo Loas. Recently, I took a spiritual pilgrimage to New Orleans, to be on the land, to walk the streets of my spiritual ancestors. I meditated by swamp waters to connect with the spirits of Runaway slaves like St. Marron and John the conqueror. I asked the spirits to "Tell me how to honor you?"

My spiritual practice now is more eclectic yet more culturally grounded and honest. On Monday, I light a candle and ask Papa Legba to open the door to spirits world. Then on nature sabbats, I return to my Wicca practice. I am honoring all parts of myself. I'm the person who wants to dance with nature and with Yemaya. I'm the person who wants magic to rule over her life. I am the girl who wants to be engulfed in her culture, her people and be held by the spirits. Yes, I am trying to have it all. I am rejecting the notions that Black Americans are not allowed to have anything. We are rejected from Africa and America. We are taught that we have no home. But, I am taking control of my life and path. I am finding my place and home in all these places regardless of what the world thinks I deserve.

Wounded Healer (Cultural Trauma Ritual)

Possible Setting: Anywhere near a body of water and Trees

Tools: No decoration except small potted plants (enough for every participant). Also have towels for drying feet.

Cleansing

To begin this ritual everyone will be asked to bathe their feet in the water.

Facilitator: In Guinea there is a tradition of bathing one's feet after a visit to slave dungeons because dungeons are consecrated with blood and pain. Cleansing one's feet helps them to release all the suffering they touched by walking along the dungeons. Cleansing feet is of course a wonderful custom in many religions including Christianity. Today, we use the symbol to acknowledge our own suffering and that of our ancestors that have yet to be healed. [1]

Take a few moments to let the water touch and wash over your own sense of woundness, and whenever you are ready. (Take your time). You can dry your feet.

After everyone is done with the feet washing, they are instructed to find an object that represents their woundness or what they are working towards healing.

Opening

Facilitator: Once everyone has found an object please gather in a circle and place the object by your side.

---

[1] Inspiration for this ritual came in part from a racial oppression weekend intensive with Belvie Rooks and Tom Dewolf. Belvie discussed feet bathing after a trip to the slave dungeons. She also read to us the Alice Walker "torture" poem which will be used later in this ritual.

Everyone gathers in a circle.
Now if you are comfortable doing so, can we all take hands. As we hold hands may this be an affirmation that in this circle no one is alone, that everyone here will be supportive of each other in this journey towards healing. Please repeat after me:
"We are not alone.
My Community
My Ancestors
My circle will be my strength".
You can now release hands

Invocating

Facilitator: Let us begin with a prayer and affirmation
This journey has weakened us, guided us away from our homes, the blood of our ancestors still haunt us, How spirit do we feel our way home? This earth raped like the endless bodies of women. The spirit blinded by the horrors of humankind, how can we heal? There seem to be no hope, endless troubles await but we wash our wounds, we bathe in this muck. So we can dance, praise and laugh in this fire. We will walk on; thrive regardless of what storms follow. Recreating our home in winds, waves, tree and stars. Never lost because the spirit reminds us that our names live in everything. And our ancestors hold us all up, they are the very ground beneath our tired feet. May we always remember this. That a wounded warrior is no less a warrior. May the spirit always and the ancestors always be with us. May we never forget who we truly are and what we are meant to be.
Amen, Blessed Be, So it is.
We will gather in this place with the goal of healing through honesty, compassion. May we invoke the principles of community, nonviolence and Truth telling. May our ancestors, our families and all our peoples who cannot be here in body, be here in spirit.

Witnessing

Facilitator: Now we will go around the circle, pick up our object and say one word that describes the pain that we are ready to release or acknowledge. *After you have said your word please place the rock in the middle. If you do not have a word just place the object in silence.*

Everyone places their object and we have an altar of pain, suffering and trauma.

Let's take a moment in silence to bear witness to the altar of our wounds. As we must be willing to look at the truth of the past, no matter how horrible, to move forward.

Silence

Healing

Facilitator: Now turn to a partner and both of you will attempt to answer the question of, "What would healing look like?"

Afterwards, everyone turns back to the larger group and is asked to say one word that describes healing to you.

Facilitator: Pick up an object (yours or someone else's) and when you are ready walk over to the water and place the object in the water. As you watch the object move away know that everything can be transformed and reused by the earth in different ways. We can choose to be abusers because we were wounded or be wounded healers.

Grounding

Afterwards, people return to the circle and everyone is handed a small potted plant.

Facilitator: This plant that may seem separated from its natural state, still maintains its roots, its sense of home and wholeness. Maybe this can be a symbol of your continuous growth because regardless of separation, trauma, what life brings us or when death comes, we all return home.

Closing

Facilitator reads Alice Walker's Poem "Torture" or similar poem:

Cecily Joy Willowe, M.Div

When they torture your mother
plant a tree
when they torture your father
plant a tree
When they torture your brother
and your sister
plant a tree
When they assassinate
your leaders
and lovers
plant a tree
Whey they torture you
too bad
to talk
plant a tree.
When they begin to torture
the trees
and cut down the forest
they have made
start another.

We now thank our Ancestors, family and friends who have joined us in spirit within this circle. And may the work we have done today be for their benefit and our own. May the healing and inspiration inside this circle remain with us as we return to our everyday lives.

References

Walker, A. (2005). In search of our mothers' gardens, womanist prose. (p. xi). Mariner Books.
Walker, A "Torture." Retrieved from
http://www.poemhunter.com/poem/torture-26/

Loving My Blackness: A Personal Reflection

Crystal Blanton

I love the way my natural hair curls; twisting and turning into a pattern of beauty and wonder. Each day the curls tell a different story, unpredictable and yet defined in excellence.

I love how my skin is a mixture of the history of my past. It is the color of the trauma of rape, and yet is the symbol of resilience. It is the color of a revolutionary, and an agent for change.

I love how my history shows fierceness from the experience of warriors, healers, mothers, fathers, kings, queens, slaves, and visionaries. It is within the path of their pain that I have been born into a life of potential.

I love that my culture teaches me humility. The sacrifice of millions teaches me to be grateful for what I have and humble in my understanding of survival.

I love the intensity that is encoded in my DNA and courses through the blood within my veins. I see the immense drive to persevere within my ancestor's stories, and I know that I too have been born with the DNA of legends.

I love the depth of the Black spirit. It is often indescribably deep, connected to unconscious transgenerational knowledge that is not always taught but felt.

I love the fullness of my lips, reminding me to connect with the sensations of life and love. It is through these lips that I kiss my partner and that I encourage my children. My speech is full, and my love is whole.

I love the shadow of my Blackness, for it is a part of my ancestral pride. The shadow of our past has always been the motivating fuel for our future. We are stronger than imaginable, and connected in strength through a shared lineage of pain. It is the balance of the dark and the light that illuminates from the resilience of our past; in partnership with one another.

Don't feel sorry for my Blackness, it is a source of pride. It is not something I am ashamed of or scared to embrace, it is my ancestors mark on my visual soul. I wear it like a badge; showing that I will always be protected by the strength of the survivors before me, cloaked in the brilliance of color.

Don't be afraid of my power, we cannot change the world if we are afraid of the brilliance within one another.

Don't be afraid to hear my Black pride, it is not meant to take away from yours. It is within my connection to my culture that I can truly respect and love who *you* are too.

Don't run from my history, it is yours too, and together we can learn to write the future.

It is our collective Blackness and our Whiteness, our brown and our tan, our history and our present, our hopes and our fears, our pain and our joys, our dreams and our future that we are working for together.

TOGETHER.

The Many Faces of Athena

Heaven Walker

Introduction

Athena has often been perceived primarily as the Greek Goddess of War and Wisdom. Although she is viewed as a powerful female deity she is portrayed by Greek dramatists as an avid supporter of patriarchal culture. "There is no mother who gave birth to me and I approve the male principle in all things... (Aeschylus, 657-667)." However, her mythology has been recorded primarily by men who had a vested interest in using her image to support male supremacy. There are many faces of Athena and one must peel away the layers of misogynistic thought to truly understand this Goddess and reclaim her matriarchal identity as a Goddess of women's liberation and freedom. In the process of unraveling the identity of Athena, we are also confronted with the knowledge that the origins of Athena are in North Africa and that her Black origins have been suppressed. I give thanks to Martin Bernal, who has now passed from this incarnation for bringing this truth to light through his book *"Black Athena."*

Athena's Origins

In popular mythology Athena's birth is a triumph for patriarchal society, as she is born without the aid of a woman. The sky God Zeus swallows Athena's mother Metis and Athena springs forth from Zeus's head fully armored, and fully grown. This myth is not questioned, and neither is Athena's Greek heritage. However, there is a submerged belief that Athena is actually from Africa. In *Black Athena* Martin Bernal presents evidence that "Hellenistic culture" or Classical civilization has Afroasiatic roots. He also states that even the classical Greeks themselves were aware that philosophy, religion, and many other parts of their culture originated from Egypt.

In regards to Athena, the patron deity of the Greek capitol city, Bernal traces her roots back to Egypt and Libya. Bernal points out that there are great similarities between Athena and the Egyptian Goddess Nt or Neit. In fact, The Ancients saw Athena and Neit as the same goddess (Bernal, 52). Both Neit and Athena were virgin goddesses of wisdom, weaving, and warfare. He also points out that the cult of Neit was centered in the city of Sais, whose inhabitants felt a special affinity for the Athenians.

Sais was located on the frontier of Egypt and Libya and was sometimes part Libyan (Bernal, 52). The religious title of the city of Sais was Ht Nt which means temple of Neit. Furthermore, the vocalization of Ht Nt would sound something like "Atanait" which is very close to "Athena (Bernal, 50-51)."

Lucia Chiavola-Birnbaum also alludes to the African origins of Hellenism when she mentions Marie Durand-Lefebvre's discovery that classical Greco-Roman writers described Isis, Cybele, Diana, Hera, and Dionysus; all prominent Egyptian or Greek gods, as black (Birnbaum, 136). This statement corroborates Bernal's statement that even the classical Greeks understood that their religion derived from a "black" source.

Lucia also discusses the shared values of dark woman divinities. She references a postcard that was sent to her by Michele Radford that described the similarities of the rituals performed for the Black Madonna's of Europe and the rituals performed to honor Kali. Kali is lit up with neon lights and is paraded through the streets and then brought to the river for a ritual bath. Black Madonnas are also honored in this way (Birnbaum, 123).

Patricia Monaghan describes a similar festival to honor Athena in her book *The Goddess Path*. The Summer Solstice festival of Athens involved taking an image of Athena from the Acropolis, parading it through the streets, taking it to the sea, bathing it ceremoniously to renew strength and purity, and then clothing it in a new robe that was made specifically for the occasion (Monaghan, 51). The similarities of the Athenian Summer Solstice ceremony, the ceremony honoring Kali, and the many ceremonies honoring Black Madonna's leads me to the conclusion that all three are dark woman divinities, in essence, black.

Barbara Walker seems to agree with Bernal about Athena's African origins. She refers to "Athene" as the Libyan triple Goddess Neith, Metis, Medusa...who came from North Africa (Walker, 74). Zsuzsanna Budapest also claims that Athena is an African Goddess that was whitened "considerably" by the Greeks (Budapest, 280). C. Osbourne also speaks of Athena's African origins in her academic article "Amazon Nation: A Sourcebook" and claims that Athena was an Amazon born from Lake Tritonis in Libya (Osborne).

Athena's Identity as Warrior and Supporter of Patriarchy

If Athena was born in or around Lake Tritonis, this presents a challenge to the popular Greek myth that Athena sprang from Zeus's head. There are actually many creation stories of Athena. However, her masculinized birth is the myth that is most widely accepted and connects her to a war-like identity. It is quite possible that her warrior aspect has nothing to do with patriarchal warfare. Her warrior aspect very well could be the last remaining vestige of an Amazon identity. The name "Amazon" is a Greek name for Goddess-worshipping tribes in North

Africa, Anatolia and the Black Sea. Scholars now say that the word "Amazon" may have meant "moon – woman." Libya, where it is suspected that Athena was born, was Amazonian. Herodotus spoke of Libyan Amazons and called the Amazons *the war-like women of Libya*. (Walker, 25)."

According to myth, Theseus, the king of Attica "violated the Amazons law of matrifocal marriage by kidnapping their queen who was variously named Hippolyta, Antiope, or Melnippe (Black Mare)." The Amazons raided Greece, ravaged coastal towns, and invaded Athens. This put the Amazons and Greeks at odds with each other and made them sworn enemies. In fact, according to legend the Amazons hated the Greeks so much that they came to the aid of matriarchal Troy during the Trojan War (Walker, 24-25).

In The *New Book of Goddesses & Heroines* Patricia Monaghan tells us a little bit more about the inner workings of Amazonian societies. According to the Greeks the Amazons lived on the borders of Greece and mated once a year with the men from nearby tribes. The daughters were kept and the men were crippled, killed, or most likely, returned to their villages of origin.

Amazonian society consisted of two major leaders or queens. One queen was in charge of defense and the other was in charge of domestic affairs. Under the guidance of the military queen the Amazons were a formidable army of mounted warriors with ivy shaped shields and double-bladed axes or the "labrys" which interestingly enough is the symbol associated with the lesbian feminist movement. Under the rule of the domestic queen the Amazons lived peacefully together, were economically self sufficient, and thrived artistically (Monaghan, 43).

Osbourne links Athena's Amazonian origins to the Gorgon Medusa. She suggests that the Gorgons were one of the most famous Amazonian tribes in Libya.

Furthermore, she states that Medusa is not a monster at all, but the original Libyan Amazonian maiden form of Athena. If Medusa/Athena were of North African origin than it is possible the "snakes" on Medusa's head were in fact dreadlocks, which is a spiral like hairstyle that was reportedly worn by the Hamitic people of North Africa as well as many other African cultures. According to Greek mythology, Athena helped the Greek hero Perseus to slay Medusa. This act glorifies Athena's patriarchal warrior aspect. Any man who looked directly upon one of the Gorgons would immediately turn to stone. Athena helped Perseus by holding up her shield, or in some versions a mirror, so that Perseus could see Medusa's reflection in order to slay her without looking directly upon her (Hamilton, 151).

Susan Carter presents a varying opinion about this myth. She suggests that Athena holds up the shield so that Perseus may look upon his own reflection, not Medusa's (Carter, 214). Even in her patriarchal aspect Athena is labeled the God of war *and* wisdom. Perhaps Athena thought it unwise to slay Medusa, which propagates violence against women, and gave him the "mirror" to look deep within himself and reflect on his decision. If this were the case, metaphorically speaking, Athena gave Perseus the chance to change the course of history and the progression of patriarchy. Unfortunately, he does not rise to this challenge and slays Medusa. His actions illustrate a patriarchal standard that condones violence against women that is still being played out in our current day culture.

Although Athena's warrior aspects are highly emphasized in popular mythology she has other aspects that are also important in discerning her true identity. In her book *The Goddess Path* Patricia Monaghan gives detailed descriptions of the meanings of many different goddesses, of which Athena is included. Monaghan provides an in depth description of Athena's identity as a household Goddess. Athena symbolized the family bond and ruled over domestic crafts such as spinning, weaving and pottery (Monaghan, 50).

Athena was symbolized by the "home and the hearth-and by the mild serpent who, like a household cat, lived in the storehouse and protected the family's food supply against destructive rodents. This imagery connects Athena with the bare breasted Cretan snake goddess (Monaghan, 50-51)." C. Osboune also states that the priestesses of Athena were skilled craftswomen and snake handlers who tended the sacred serpents living by the doors of Athena's shrines and in wheat storage bins (Osbourne).

Athena and Virginity

Traditional descriptions of the Goddess Athena center around the fact that she is a maiden or virgin Goddess. Francesca De Grandis describes the virgin aspect of the Goddess as "unspoiled sexuality in all its freshness (De Grandis, 60)." The term "Unspoiled Sexuality" has many possible meanings. However in our current society unspoiled sexuality tends to have one clear cut meaning.

The word "virgin" stems from the Latin word *virgo* which means "intact (McCoy, 79)." Patriarchal religion and culture define virginity as having a hymen, (a thin membrane that covers the opening of the vagina), that is "intact." The hymen is often broken during first sexual intercourse and is therefore associated with "virginity." Even today, first sexual intercourse is referred to in popular culture as "losing your virginity" However it is interesting to note that it is possible for the hymen to break in a number of non-sexual ways such as playing sports, routine medical examination, or the insertion of a tampon.

There has been far too much focus on this little piece of skin, which has produced a fear among young women of sexual relation. They are told by older women, or popular culture, that "losing your virginity" is a painful and bloody experience. Often times, they are also told that the only person they can entrust with this horrific experience is their future husband.

The original term used to describe the virgin was *virgo intacta* which referred to the whole woman, and not just her hymen. *Virgo Intacta* was a woman who was whole unto herself. She did not need a male partner to acknowledge her worth or status. She was free to mate with anyone she chose, and often was a priestess who engaged in sex as a sacred ritual dedicated to the Goddess (McCoy, 80). In fact, "the function of *holy virgins* was to dispense the Mother's grace through sexual worship; to heal; to prophesy; to perform sacred dances; to wail for the dead; and to become Brides of God (Walker, 1049)."

The concept of virginity in our current day culture is interesting indeed. The stress of the importance of virginity serves many aspects of the patriarchal system. First and foremost it supports the patrilineal system of our culture. If a woman saves her "virginity" for her husband and only engages in sex with one man, the paternity of his children is indefinite and they are added to his lineage, receiving his last name. Patriarchal religions such as Christianity support this practice by dubbing fornication, or sex outside of marriage as a sin. What most people do not know is that in biblical times the term "virgin" was not used to describe a woman who had never been sexually active. In his book The Historical Mary, Michael Jordan states that "Among Babylonian texts detailing religious convention and morality, discovered in the Assyrian city of Nineveh, there is some salutary advice on marriage (Jordan, 171)." The text reads:

Mary not the virgin whose lovers are many...
She will not lift thee from thy sorrows,
She will ridicule thee in thy quarrels [with her]

Fear and Humility are not with her.
If she comes into a house, lead her away
If her attention be turned toward a stranger's house,
It shall be the undoing of that house,
And he that marries her shall not prosper

Jordan than goes on to say that "a virgin did not necessarily describe a chaste woman but an independent, feisty spirit. One of the clearest illustrations of the sense in which the term was applied can be found in the descriptions of the Canaanite Goddess Anat, the sister of Baal. Anat is described as "a lady of considerable sexual prowess who "makes love by the thousand" yet in the same context she is identified as "the virgin Anat (Jordan, 172)." This is quite interesting, because "Anat" is quite similar to "Anatha" and Robert Graves suggests that "Athena" is a derivative of "Anatha"(Graves, 371).

There is another aspect of Athena's "virginity" that is not often mentioned. When we think of a woman who is a "virgin" by traditional standards, we think of a woman who has not had sexual intercourse with a man. A woman's sexual practice may consist of intercourse with a man; but sexual expression is not limited to this particular act. Women can express their sexuality without the act of intercourse and are capable of many types of sexual expression with men and other women.

In The Holy Book of Women's Mysteries, Z. Budapest states that Athena is a maiden Goddess who never consorts with men; and maiden Goddesses were lesbian. She states that "sexuality in the matriarchies emphasized pleasure rather than procreation" and that "lesbianism was a natural mode of interaction among women...while heterosexuality was chosen seasonally for the purpose of breeding or attraction for men (Budapest, 280)." She also states that "lesbian sexual practices were also employed to dispel evil, to heal and prophesy, to make rain, and to raise any kind of energy necessary at any given time (Budapest, 157)."

There may be hidden traces of Athena's lesbian identity in popular mythology. An example of this is the myth of Pallas and Athena. Z. Budapest adopts the traditional myth with a feminist twist. She claims that Pallas was Athena's best friend and fell from a cliff during their Amazonian games. Athena attached Pallas's image to her breast and placed her name in front of her own becoming Pallas Athena, as a sign of love and mourning (Budapest, 280).

However, C. Osbourne suggests that Pallas and Athena were lovers and that Pallas was "killed off" in the myth to hide Athena's lesbian identity (Osbourne). If Athena and Pallas were lovers, it makes sense that "upon her death" Athena took Pallas's name and identity. If Athena was in fact a lesbian Goddess then she would fit the patriarchal definition of a virgin. Lesbian sexual practices are multifaceted and do not focus on intercourse as the primary sex act.

Whether Athena had male lovers, female lovers, or both, it is clear that she was not the sexless individual that is portrayed in popular mythology. Personally, I like the ambivalence of Athena's sexuality, because it makes her accessible to women of all sexualities.

Conclusion

Athena has a very ambiguous identity. Her origins appear not only to be from Libya, but also from an Amazonian tribe. Even if Athena was originally the Egyptian Neit as Bernal claims, Egypt is still in Africa and affirms Athena's African origins. In popular mythology Athena's strongest aspects seem to be as warrior and household domestic goddess. I find this extremely interesting as the Amazons are described as having two queens who ruled over two different aspects of the society, military and domestic. It is also clear that Athena was not a virgin goddess by any means. She may have had male lovers, female lovers, or both.

Athena's many faces represent freedom. Her multiple identities show us the many choices we have as women today. She reaches out to the maiden's, mothers, and crones of the world with one message: Love thyself, For Thou Art Goddess.

A Ritual of Freedom Dedicated to Athena

Ritual Tools

Olive oil, 3 green Olives, a piece of black string or thread long enough to make three knots, a pencil, 2 pieces of paper, a red pen, a small figurine or statue of a woman that symbolizes you, a red candle and something to light it with, and a pot of water

Ritual

Anoint your third eye, with a drop of olive oil and take a moment to meditate on the meaning of Athena. Athena is the Goddess of wisdom, the arts, and most of all freedom. What does it mean to be free? What does it mean to be "a woman unto herself?" What has held you back from being free? Or from being whole? Are their negative thought patterns that you have fallen into such as self doubt, insecurity, helplessness, fear? Are there current relationships in your life that contribute to these feelings? Now pick up your pencil and a piece of paper and write these things down. Take your time, and allow yourself to write everything that comes into your head, do not censor anything. Now light the red candle and roll the piece of paper into a scroll. Take the black string and tie it around the scroll, knotting it three times. As you do this, think about how different your life might be if you banished these things from your life. Ask Athena for her assistance in helping you banish these things. Now light the paper on fire with the flame of the candle. As the paper burns visualize the things on the paper vanishing from your life. If this is difficult, take the first step by visualizing the words vanishing from the paper. Now pick up your statuette or figurine, bathe her in the pot of water and say "In the name of Athena I purify and cleanse myself of all things that no longer serve me. I am strong, I am whole, and I am free." Now pick up your pen and write three things that you can do to promote a sense of freedom and wholeness. Now eat the three olives one by one. With every olive you eat, speak out loud each of the things that you have written on your paper and one by one visualize yourself doing these things. Now close by saying "Athena, patron and defender of women, help me to stay my course, to be true to myself, and to always strive for freedom, Blessed Be."

Bibliography

Primary Sources
Aeschuylus. Eumenides.Trans. A.J. Podlecki. Warminster, England: Aris & Phillips Ltd.,1989.
Bernal, Martin. Black Athena: The Afroasiatic Roots of Classical Civilization. New Brunswick, New Jersey: Rutgers University Press, 1987.
Budapest, Zsuzsanna. The Holy Book of Women's Mysteries. Berkeley, CA: Wingbow Press, 1989.
Carter, Susan. *Athena and the Mirror* from SheIs Everywhere: An Anthology of Womanist/Feminist Spirituality, Edited by Lucia Chiavola-Birnbaum. Lincoln, NE:iUniverse,Inc.,2005.
Chiavola – Birnbaum, Lucia. Dark Mother: African Origins and Godmothers. Lincoln, NE: Authors Choice Press, 2001.
Conway, D. J. Wicca: The Complete Craft. St. Paul MN: Llewellyn Publications, 2001.
De Grandis, Francesca. Be a Goddess! A Guide to Celtic Spells and Wisdonm for Self-Healing, Prosperity and Great Sex. San Francisco, CA: Harper San Francisco,

1998.
Graves, Robert. The White Goddess: A Historical Grammar of Poetic Myth. New York, NY: Farrar, Straus and Giroux, 1948.
Jordan, Michael. The Historical Mary: Revealing the Pagan Identity of the Virgin Mother. Berkeley, CA: Seastone, 2003.
Hamilton, Edith. Mythology: Timeless Tales of Gods and Heroes. New York, NY: Warner Books, Inc.,1942.
McCoy, Edain. Celtic Women's Spirituality: Accessing the Cauldron of Life. St. Paul, MN: Llewellyn Publications, 1998.
Monaghan, Patricia. The New Book of Goddesses & Heroines. St.Paul, MN: Llewellyn Publications, 1997.
Monaghan, Patricia. The Goddess Path. St. Paul, MN: Llwellyn Publications, 1999.
Walker, Barbara. The Woman's Encyclopedia of Myths and Secrets. San Francisco, CA: Harper San Francisco, 1983.

Secondary Sources

"Chapter 7: Athena" The Amazon Nation: A Sourcebook 2000-2012 C. Osborne
(http://www.moonspeaker.ca/Amazons/PartTwo/chapterseven.html)

The Other Southerner

Dr. Katharyn Privett-Duren
(Seba O'Kiley)

"She had an inside and an outside now and suddenly she knew how not to mix them."

Zora Neale Hurston, Their Eyes Were Watching God

"An Indian is an Indian regardless of the degree of Indian blood or which little government card they do or do not possess."

Wilma Mankiller

My magic, my Tribe and my feet are all embedded deep within the Bible Belt of Alabama. And it's complicated. If you saw me sauntering down the street with my chopped black hair, native features and cream skin, you wouldn't think: witch, Cherokee, Apache, African American.[2] No, I pass for the other heritage in my blood that runs thicker than red mud in the lower half of our state: Irish (or *Scots-Irish*). Even this legacy is a muddled version of the island folk from which so many of us hail: for an Alabamian is expected to trace their family trees that far, yet never to allow them to trace back. *That* legacy, along with slavery and the Trail of Tears, is to be noted only in stage whispers behind hands around Sunday suppers. I reside here. I practice here. I was born here. And I am passing.[3]

---

[2] My father was of Arizona Apache origin, a strange warrior mix with my maternal Cherokee line, and my family tree is ripe with African American grandmothers.

[3] In academic studies, "passing" usually holds racial context. Here, I am using it as a lens through which to view both race and religious identity.

There's an innate sense of guilt in my bones for passing as "one of them" and it haunts me. I've wondered what my fellow Alabamians would think if they knew, sitting next to a non-Anglo witch at the annual Syrup Soppin' or sharing barbeque with me at the Waverly 280 Boogie, my toes tapping next to theirs. Christianity and whiteness are assumed here if you look like me.[4] I doubt if my African American friends from the AME would still hold my hand if they could see me in front of a cauldron, athame held against a night sky, dancing in bare feet and utter abandon. I am subtly "othered" in ways that make me homesick, even when (because?) my toes are stained red with local clay.[5] And then? There's the "other" thing: I am highly educated. That doctorate on the wall is signed by the same governor I vote against, every time, and is a brutal affront to my own slow, Southern drawl. In effect, everything I *am* stands (at first glance) in diametric opposition to whole of my environment. That is, if we can ignore legacy.

While I pass, evading burning crosses, unemployment and an inheritance of torment for my children, my existence here is wholly sanctioned. We (my Tribe and I) are the echo of what came before: Cherokee grandmothers, African American matriarchs and Scots/Irish farmers who all understood magic as integral to a whole and healthy existence.[6] Their memories, dances, foods and worship vibrate so strong in our bones

---

[4] And for this, I feel guilt, too.
[5] There are multiple definitions and uses of the concept of "othering" in academic studies. This one in particular seems pertinent here: "The development and maintenance of every culture requires the existence of another different and competing alter ego. The construction of identity... whether Orient or Occident, France or Britain... involves establishing opposites and otherness whose actuality is always subject to the continuous interpretation and reinterpretation of their differences from us." Said, E. (1995) *Orientalism: Western Conceptions of the Orient*, (revised edition), London: Penguin: 332.
[6] The Cherokee word for wellness is "tohi," a term that encompasses the health of the mind, body and spirit. If one part is sick, all parts are out of balance.

that we risk identity capture in order to preserve our heritage. And we do so, every day that we breathe. To be Southern is to be private, already: we dare not speak of our secrets. It is simply *not done*. To be "witch" and Southern means a doubling of the veil, a thickening of our code that protects our ways and their authenticity. Even here, I tread on hallowed ground.

My tribe is a family tradition—that oft belittled vein of Paganism born of lineage, blood and time. While others may hold papers to their legitimacy, our tribal names are written in a family grimoire of sorts and remembered to our children. To be *Gangani* means to hold to the olden ways of *our* specific peoples, to honor our land, to revere the art of storytelling and to pass down those sacred customs that sustained our ancestors. Within a season, tables are strewn in dried gourds and corn porridges from a Celtic Mabon feast until our beloved Cherokee Ripe Corn Ceremony. In effect: we are a makeshift coven of natives, tribal in our ways, reaching back to our roots and crafting lives that honor them. And so, while our existence might be met with horror by our local Baptist church, it is *sanctioned* by the spirit of this land. I see my fellow Alabamians stomp wood with abandon ("clogging") and wonder if they realize its Scots-Irish origins? Or that the original design for the banjo was conceptualized by African slaves? That the thick attachment to land in our region was born of non-Nomadic Cherokees and poverty-stricken (often outlawed or indebted) Irish folk? These are our ancestors. Their voices are in the whine of winter against pine trees and in the deep rumble of Celtic, Cherokee and the displaced African magic of our rivers. I suppose, then, that we are only *othered* by and through the falsity of progress and civilization.

And of course, by Bible Belt Christianity.

Still, we remain. Initiated only as family, the Gangani Tribe holds to the Irish/Celtic traditions of the region from which we hail, as well as that of our Cherokee bloodlines.[7] We are Southern tribal "witch mutts," spinning and turning the wheel well under the Mason Dixon Line. Such a practice insists on what most might consider inconvenience. For us, it's a way of life. Why, I would no more throw the bones of a roasted chicken in the trash than I would my wooden spoon. Such an act is a dishonor to the living animal that should be revered and utilized — blood to bone. Our herbs are heritage plants nursed from seed to dried; our peppers and beans are aged on the stalk and harvested by the moon. It's a native theology once held by the people who truly cultivated homesteads and worshipped upon this land. This practice — one that upholds and respects the primacy of earthly cycles — once nourished our people before processed foods and super stores pillaged our memories. We are, in many ways, ghosts here: pressing our own wine, culling hay for chicken beds, recycling the products of Mother Earth like haints of a time that our fellow Southerners have forgotten.

As Southern (organized) Paganism pales in contrast to that of the rest of the country, and as we hold to secrecy in order to preserve the sanctity of our tradition, we are quite alone in our faith here in the trees. Our neighbors put up mangers and brightly lit crosses while we howl around our ritual Yule fire. Our downtown is adorned with "Put Christ Back in Christmas" signs framed in tinsel while we busily craft candles, wooden talking sticks and sage bundles to show our love to our Tribe. Only at Samhain do we blend in at the pumpkin carvings as good Baptists don their black witch hats made in China, unaware that they are in the company of real witchcraft. *Native, ancient witchcraft.* And perhaps they do know the truth, somewhere under their coifed hair and Mary Kay makeup.

---

[7] My family tree that branches away from native blood lands squarely upon the banks of the Gangani River and in the lap of an ancient Celtic Tribe (Γαγγανοι) related to the Kingdom of Gwynedd.

I hear them at parties wondering at my high cheekbones, tracing my dark eyebrows with their eyes, marveling at the hair turning paint white instead of European gray, wanting to touch the tribal necklace that hangs around my neck with their manicured fingers. Perhaps, I'm not passing at all, but only complying.

And while our zip code, birth certificates and land taxes all name the same state, as a witch among my Alabama brethren I am *still* wearing a mask of civilized compliance. My feet long to stomp around fire, my heart breaks at the sight of budding corn and aches for living soil covered in steel ash and mini-mall concrete. In my howl, far out into the country, something uncivilized longs to reclaim itself. I awkwardly reach for fellowship in technological forums of my witch kin and find that something is lost without the scent of skin. Even then, my faith doesn't fit neatly into popular Pagan factions; regionality and family trads rarely situate squarely in the lingo. I suppose here, in the Pagan world, I am othered, too.

Still, it occurs to me that *to be othered* does not mean *to be inauthentic*. In fact, it is often quite the opposite. Sanctioning of the self has little to do with community acceptance, or with its tolerance, for that matter. Shall I accept whiteness as my designation, if only because I look white? Shall I accept my Pagan community's disregard for my tradition, if only because it does not hold papers in England? Iceland? Shall I *other* myself?

Perhaps I shall. My sister is fond of telling me: "No one thinks like you." And I suppose, few still do. I am a relic of my great-grandmother who could not speak English and sat perfectly still, braids of white coiling upon her dark neck. Yet, I am also the descendant of a matriarchal people who saw "God" as a woman. *I am a witch*, spiraling and turning in the boondocks of Alabama, no shirt/no shoes required. My DNA is no stranger to this

land, but my tribal existence most assuredly *is* in 2014.
I am? *Other.* So mote it be.

Seba

Warrior Witch[8]

On the verge of manhood in a Christian town
He walks flat-footed to feel the ground
A memory in flesh and sacred bone
An ancestor's sacrifice stomps alone
Fluorescent lights bruise and crisp his skin
Where sunlight should assuage the sin
Only dusk can salve the ache
When masks are dropped and roles escaped
He howls against the thud of time
The witch, the warrior, this child of mine.
As aether swells to meet his tread
Into the twilight, I am led
To taste the dust of coppered feet
Forgotten, remembered against moss and peat
But then he kneels, embraced in pine
And in Her arms, becomes entwined
The witch, the warrior,
This child of mine.

---

[8] The following is a poem I wrote at the formal initiation of my son, Atsila Waya.

The Magic of Memory: Authentic Ancestral Exchange

Crystal Blanton

Memories hold powerful magic inside of them. Although we don't usually think of our minds as the holder of our magical wisdom, it is the most magical book of shadows that a person can have. The secrets of our lessons are often stored within our memories. It is for this reason that feelings of love and fear can be recalled in an instant, moments from the past that holds enough power to evoke feelings.

Memories are like time release capsules that titrate our lessons over time. I try not to ignore the memories that come to me, even when they are unpleasant, because of this gained understanding that pieces of my future self are stored within that magic. It has become abundantly clear that how we connect, perceive and integrate the memories of our past actively shapes the stones that we step on to develop the future. Secret knowledge from the collective memory of our family and ancestors are passed down energetically through generations; I unknowingly hold those secrets too. Until recently I never thought about the energetic familial lineage that I have been connected to my whole life. Why would I think that the stories and memories of my people's past would be a part of who I am, or who I am to become? How could I possibly retain some of the knowledge and wisdom of those I had never met?

A fellow counselor I used to work with would always say, "Understanding is just the booby prize", and this saying reflects what I have come to truly understand. I don't know how this is true, even though I have theories, but I do know that it is so. I see this truth when I look at my son, and what he inherently knows that I have not taught him. I am beginning to see it within myself as well; in my knowing of things I was not formally taught.

When we, as human beings, stop limiting our abilities by the confines of what is "possible" or seen, we might stop questioning our ability to be greater than we can imagine. Once we achieve the ability to see beyond our perceived capacity, then we can focus our love and attention into the future of who we are, and ways to bring that knowledge to the surface. The ability to evolve can heal all wounds. Imagine who we might all become. Imagine a level of healing that would connect the wounds of our ancestral past and roads that will lead to our children's futures.

If knowledge is power, then our memories are the power box that holds all the wires safely inside. The very memories of those things I have experienced, and the transgenerational memories of those things I hold, are all important to my personal power, freedom and spiritual insight.

Ritualizing the sacred processes in our lives can indeed add significance to the seemingly mundane activities of life, so I have chosen to honor my personal and ancestral memories as a sacred and divine tool. In my home we have an ancestor altar up all year long; it is a part of the sacred ancestral exchange. We honor and hold space for those who came before us, and the reciprocal relationship between our mighty dead and our ancestral lessons. We are also working on a social justice altar in honor of all those who have fought for equality, honoring the sacred connection between our freedoms and their sacrifices.

As a means to reinforce the bond between our ancestors of bone and blood, and those of heart and soul, we tell stories, we talk about our past, we share our research, and we are honest about our personal and cultural struggles and accomplishments. We create rituals and traditions in our holidays, our cooking and our lifestyle. Our authentic memories mix with the exchange of magic new and old, and we manifest beauty.

I still cook the same dishes at Thanksgiving as my mother did, and as her mother did before. The repetitive and consistent nature of celebration in our recipes creates a flavor to our magic that cannot be described to others; it is ours, it is our families, and it came from our ancestors. It's a powerful combination that is not always recognized as magic, but it is.

When I am cooking the greens, corn bread, and yams at this specific time every year, I feel as if my soul is transported to a time in which I could not possibly remember. A time when my grandmother would wear her stockings and slippers in the kitchen, cooking with pots all over the stove, and dishes on that long wood dining room table. I feel a familiar confidence that permeates my being, knowing by sight just how much of each ingredient to put in. And when we eat there is a moment of contentment that feels like we are wrapped in the arms of a huge love that we cannot quite conceptualize; it is an unknowing love in this physical plane.

It is a common occurrence for me to cry at a moment during Thanksgiving because these magical memories evoke such feeling and emotion inside of me. Since the death of my mother, this feeling of unconditional love that comes from my family's collective and magical memories help to hold me rooted in my familial foundation.

Instead of fighting these moments out of fear of feeling too much, or being distracted from the present, I add them into my experience of oneness with my magic. This integration and acknowledgement is a part of the spell that releases the magic so that it may flow. Several recent studies, including one done by Dias Ressler that was published in Nature Neuroscience, are showing that memories are passed down on a cellular level through the lineage of generations. These studies are showing empirical data on the magic of memory that we have known as practitioners of the craft; the magic of our ancestors does not go away with the passing of life, but can gain in power and be passed down through the encoding of magical memory on future generations. Memory itself is magical; It is the imprinting of time and space, in a non-linear fashion. This type of imprinting within our mind's eye has the power of the moment in which it was created, much like a knot spell that releases magic at the time in which we choose it; memories release and hold magic within them, and within us.

Keeping with the spirit of our memories as our magical tool, I came up with a way to bless those sacred memories that I hold and those I am energetically connected to, by blessing them as I would any other magical tool:

In honor of the divine workings of the body in which I inhabit, the mind in which I hold, and the memories in which are contained, I bless the function of magic, memories, wisdom and secrets protected in this here space. May our connections forge a bridge of understanding through space and time, history and circumstance, so that I may continue the legacy of strength and magic gained by my experiences, and those of our people.

Whether I am reciting this in my bed, in my kitchen, during ritual, or in my mind, I am identifying intent for this divine vessel, and reinforcing the magical and conscious connection between myself and my ancestral magic. Some people work a lifetime to disconnect from their personal and collective story, but I am choosing to do the opposite.

The total of who I am does not begin or end with just a conscious decision of who I want to be. It is also the lines of struggle, ancestral power, collective memory of survival and strength that sits within my conscious and subconscious psyche as a result of the magical memories of those who came before me. I don't just choose to connect to myself, I also choose to connect to all that they were and are.

And then I make magic. I take these magical moments and write my thoughts, memories, connections, and feelings about what I am experiencing and what it means to me. I have this vision of handing down an inclusive memory book of writing to my children, giving them my research, my writing, spells, rituals, history and dreams. I don't want them to start over in trying to figure out who I was, and who they are. It will be more than a Book of Shadows; it will be my memories that will last throughout time and space.

One of the many tragedies of the lineage of my people, and of the African American story within history, is the lack of information passed down in first hand writing. Much of our history is written from the minds and words of those who were engaged in the oppressive systems that inflicted wounds on Black people in this country, thereby leaving transgenerational memories as one of our only authentic connection to our history.

I am embracing every moment as my ritual, every memory as my lessons, every thought as my will, and every plan as my manifestation. If our most valuable magical tool resides within us, we must remember that we are magic wherever we go, and we have the ability to manifest the strength of our people in any space and time. It is a power I am honored to hold inside of me, and one I am still learning how to use.

This Land Is Your Land

Sandra Santiago

This land is your land.
This land is my land.
But, you don't seem to understand
that we were here first.

We come from those who
speak the world into place.
Brown, skin brown
the color of earth.
Red, skin red as
the desert sand.

We were here first.

Yet this ceased to be land.
So far from home
yet so near.

First,
Taino,
Chichimeca,
Azteca,
Maya,
Tolteca,
 Later,
Fulani,
Yoruba,
Ahanti,
Congo,
Mandinka,

Sandra Santiago

We talked among ourselves
and quietly cried through
capture, survival, and disbursal.

So far from home yet so near,
is the blood of my veins,
streams in valleys
that nourished 1000
generations of villages.
It is the rhythm of that stream
that echoes throughout the hills,
where birds and tress
once sang to me,
telling me *cuentos* of
the search for *vida* and truth

Those lives have become the anthology
To a history that I now traverse,
distanced, fragmented, uprooted lost.

I am a hollowed corse carving.
I am diasporatic nations in self-exile,
carried on waves of
anonymity and yearning.
Ancestor graves cry out,
churning pieces of prophecy
in dangerous languages,
saying more of this world,
than is contained in any history book.

My Blood Song

Szmeralda Shanel

You were mine many times before now. The goddess Brigit calls to me.

My flames will transform you, my waters will heal you. The goddess Brigit calls to me.

But I am a priestess of the dark mother Auset, a daughter of Sothis.

You are my daughter too. The goddess Brigit calls to me.

But I am a priestess of the dark mother Auset, a daughter of Serpent.

I am the Serpent too. The goddess Brigit calls to me.

But I am a priestess of the sight and sacred arts

I am the fiery arrow, the illuminating light of foresight, the spark that ignites and inspires creativity. The goddess Brigit calls to me.

But I am a priestess who honors my ancestors.

I am your ancestor. The goddess Brigit calls to me.

I am an African American priestess primarily serving deities of Africa and the Diaspora. In the traditions of Africa and the Diaspora, ancestor reverence is of utmost importance. As a black person in America, living with the legacy of slavery and all that it entails it has been difficult for me to honor my European ancestors. How do I honor ancestors who most likely became ancestors by raping my other ancestors? How do I, as a priestess, honor certain ancestors while ignoring others who are also responsible for my existence?

This is the problem with being spiritual. One moment you're minding your own business, walking the path in beauty, wisdom and all that good stuff. The next moment, without clear warning, you find you are being stalked by your shadow, lurking here and there, haunting you, challenging you to look at what you thought you were beyond or at least already doing right. Don't get me wrong. I am not one who is afraid of the dark. I am a priestess of Black Isis. But when it came to facing the truth of who I am biologically and how it connects to my spiritual work and experience, things got very uncomfortable.

When I trace my ancestry back through slavery on plantations in the American south one thing is quite clear: my family's recorded history shows time and time again children born to enslaved black women and white men. Some of these men owned my ancestresses as slaves, and while others may not have owned them, they certainly were in positions that gave them the power to do as they wished with them without any consequence.

There are folks in my family who like to tell stories about possible affairs between slave and master. I am a romantic for sure, but I don't buy bullshit; a slave is property and property cannot give consent. For this reason, I am more inclined to believe what I know to be historically true: slave masters, overseers, and other white men who had access, systematically raped slaves.

I am tormented by the fact that I can trace my European ancestry back to specific countries and these ancestors have names that I know and remember. My African ancestors were enslaved and given the names of the ones who owned them. Their true names and countries of origin are lost to me. And here I stand, blood pulsing through me, DNA spiraling, humming ancient tunes from various Celtic lands. These strange soul songs, a subtle ache winding between and wrapping around the strong polyrhythmic drum songs of Mother Africa and the chant songs of the indigenous people of the American southeast. My ancestral song haunts me.

I am not ashamed of this music, but neither am I exactly proud. It is true that perhaps these white men were not all rapists, the fact still remains that many of them were. Now how do I honor all parts of my blood song?

I am stalked by my shadow, especially when the dark time of the year approaches and I start planning a feasting party for the ancestors. By candlelight we sit in circle, me and my sista priestesses (other black women who serve the goddess and the ancestors). The conversation goes like this:

"What should we do about the other ones? Should we feed them too?"

"If we do, they can't be on the same altar as our Black and Native American ancestors."

"Maybe we should just feed the women."

"Why? They owned slaves too and looked the other way when their husbands, brothers and sons raped our great-great-great grandmothers."

"Damn... It gets real when you say it like that... our great-great-great grandmothers..."

"What about further back? You know the ancestors of these ancestors, the ones who had nothing to do with slavery?"

"Fine, tonight we will feed them but on a separate altar."

Six years ago was the first Hallowe'en/Samhain I even considered acknowledging my ancestors from the British Isles.

Brigit

At first it was in small synchronistic ways in my day-to-day mundane experience that the goddess Brigit started to make herself present in my life. I would stumble across an article online or I would hear a snippet of a conversation where someone would mention Brigit, the goddess or the saint. There were times in early February, the time of her yearly celebration of Imbolc, that I would feel her energy in my home near my altar. On a few occasions I was even asked to invoke her in public Imbolc rituals. This was all fine and good. I honor and respect all goddesses and was always happy to welcome and celebrate Brigit in ritual with others. Still, I had no personal interest in committing to do any deep personal work with her.

Eventually she started to show up in very potent ways. I was looking for a teacher in the Anderson Faery/Feri tradition. I had always been interested and intrigued by Feri because, while it is a tradition with many Celtic influences and aspects, it is an American witchcraft tradition with roots in Africa and incorporates African and African diasporic elements in the teachings and practices. The day I contacted the woman who would become my teacher and initiator she said "Oh wow! I've been working with Brigit and I was just at my altar telling her I needed another female student and then you called."

Sometime later, I spent a weekend at a goddess temple where I was leading ceremony. At night and in the early morning the space was closed to visitors, and I had the temple to myself. One night when I stood in the back of the temple before my mother Isis/Auset's altar to commune with her, she sent me to the front of the temple, to Brigit's well. Why, I did not know, but I followed her instructions. I sat before Brigit's well, said a simple prayer and tossed coins into the waters. Suddenly, something loosened inside of me, a powerful force rushed through me, and I began to weep. This was the beginning.

Because I do not shed tears easily or often, I knew that while sitting at Brigit's well I had been profoundly touched by spirit and that it was time for me to do the work that I had been resisting. But for whatever reason, it took another year before I really got down to it.

One evening after having a conversation with a friend about the various aspects and intricacies of ancestor reverence, I decided I was ready to turn and face that lurking shadow head on. "Okay," I said, " I'm going to try to work with this part of my ancestry, now what?" In this moment she appeared in all her glory and brilliance, the goddess Brigit, and she said, "Start here. Start with me."

I knew some very basic things about the goddess Brigit spiritually and I made a place for her on my main altar to connect with her on a regular basis. I also felt that it was important to have a more historical and mythological understanding of her so I started to do my research. I began working daily with Brigit and she immediately sent me seeking the history, the culture and the traditions of the people who are known today as the Celts.

"Do not bother yourself with directly trying to connect with these men in your line that cause your heart anger and sadness. Ancestry is deeper than that and you do not need their stories to find what it is you are looking for. Go further back in time to the Ancient Ones, then learn what you can of the people's lore, their stories, their spirituality, their art and their music, this is how you can begin to honor this part of your heritage."

And so I began, I spoke with those who had interest and knowledge in the history, story, song, and beliefs of the Celts. I found a priestess in the Celtic spiritual tradition and became her student. I read what I could find, I prayed and I listened and everywhere I went I encountered the goddess Brigit again and again.

In the Celtic mythology she is one of the shining Tuatha Dé Danann as poetess, sage and daughter of the Dagda, the good god. I found traces of Brigit in stories of the pre-Celtic primal Goddess, the veiled hag, Cailleach. The ancient Cailleach, a Goddess associated with winter, darkness and death was said to have imprisoned a maiden called Bride who upon being rescued brought light, rebirth and the promise of spring. It is possible that this spring goddess was an earlier aspect of the Goddess who would become the Celtic triple Goddess Brigit. Again, I met the Lady, in stories of the Roman invasion of Britain, where the Brigantes, a Celtic tribe of northern England, fought under her as the martial goddess Brigga.

One evening when I was in trance, Brigit appeared to me in serpent form. I took great interest in this as many of the spirits that I serve also have this aspect. I had never read or heard anyone refer to Brigit as a serpent goddess, but as I continued my studies I eventually found that in Scottish lore she was associated with prophecy and known as the serpent queen. Brigit was so beloved by the Irish that the Catholic Church knew they were going to have a whole lot of trouble if they tried to get rid of this goddess. So we find her today still, in the symbology and mythology of Saint Bridget.

As my journey with this goddess continued through spiritual practice and research I found her presence and lore in the most surprising of all places, Haiti, where the Celtic goddess and Christian saint was adopted, transformed into a Loa and placed in the Vodun pantheon.

Maman Brigitte

"Maman Brigitte Li Soti Nan Anglete" or "Maman Brigitte she comes from England" is the beginning of a song sang in ceremony to honor this powerful Vodou spirit. Maman Brigitte is a Ghede Loa, a Loa that holds the powers of death, sexuality and fertility. She is described as a bawdy old woman who guards the cemetery. She is a Loa who heals the sick and protects women and children. Like other Ghede Loas, Maman Brigitte has a fiery tongue and is not shy about spouting obscenities. She drinks hot peppered rum and is legendary in her execution of the sexually suggestive Banda dance. Along with her husband Baron Semedi, Maman Brigitte is a guardian of the dead and leads them to the after-life.

There is some dispute about the origins of this Loa.

The song I mention says she comes from England. Some say she is the Vodou manifestation of the Celtic Brigit, and that "She comes from England" simply means she is from the British Isles.

Following the English Civil War, thousands of Irish and Scottish men and women were deported, indentured, enslaved and sent to the Caribbean islands by Cromwell's regime. And even before Cromwell's forced deportation, there were people from the British Isles immigrating to the Caribbean islands as indentured servants.

As Kerry Noonan has documented, Irish sailors arrived in the Caribbean as members of European navies, they fought on both sides of the Napoleonic wars, including the sea battles fought in the Caribbean by France and England. Many believe that in Haiti, the Irish shared their lore with the Africans and Brigit the saint was syncretized, becoming the new world Loa known today as Maman Brigitte.

Others argue that this is unlikely. I have heard Pagans of European descent say, "The characteristics and behaviors of the Loa are nothing like our lady Brigit's." In my experience, many white Pagans are afraid of and prejudiced against the religions of Africa and the Diaspora and like to make it very clear that what they are doing spiritually is nothing like what "those people over there" are doing. I have heard white Pagans explain to someone that they are a Pagan or a witch and then say, "But don't worry, I mean it's not Voodoo or anything." This could explain the resistance to any connection with the goddess Brigit and the Loa.

There are Vodouists of African descent who understandably take issue with the idea of a spirit from Europe being one of the ancestral Loa responsible for reclaiming the souls of their dead. And then there are folks from both sides who have no problem with the idea of the Loa being syncretized with the saint or Goddess but agree that there is not enough evidence to say for sure, and that this belief is a new age romantic notion at best.

Kenaz Filan, Vodou priest and author of the Haitian Vodou Handbook, says there was very little, if any, presence of Irish or English indentured servants in St.-Domingue. He argues that if there was a connection between the goddess and the Loa we would find Maman Brigitte being served in countries that had a higher percentage of indentured servants such as Jamaica or Barbados.

However, in the article **Gran Brijit: Haitian Vodou Guardian of the Cemetery,** Noonan argues that:

Priests from Brittany, the Celtic province of France, were present in Haiti both before its independence in 1804-5, and also since 1860, when Catholic priests again came to the country, for the Church had withdrawn its presence in Haiti in protest against the revolution. Catholics in both Ireland and Brittany are devoted to the Irish St. Brigit of Kildare, and many churches are dedicated to her in both areas. The influence of Irish settlers and sailors and Breton priests in spreading knowledge of St. Brigit in Haiti cannot be overstated.

People in both the Pagan and Vodou communities are concerned about spiritual appropriation and believe that the attempt to make a connection between the goddess and the Loa is just another way to sell Vodou to white Neopagans, or a way for white people who in the past have been afraid of the religion to find a way to comfortably fit in.

There are Vodou practitioners who will tell you that Maman Brigitte is usually syncretized with Mary Magdalene who is seen kneeling and holding a skull or with Saint Theresa, not Saint Brigit. And that Maman Brigitte is not another manifestation of the Celtic Brigit but of the Yoruba Orisha Oya, who like Maman Brigitte is a guardian of the dead, rules the cemetery and is also syncretized with Saint Teresa. It is even more interesting to note that in Santeria, Oya is also syncretized with our Lady of Candelaria and like Brigit, her holy day is February 2.

I understand all sides of the argument and I personally don't believe Maman Brigitte's origins are in the British Isles or in West Africa. I believe her origins are in Haiti. She is a Haitian deity with roots clearly in Africa and with fairly convincing evidence that connects her to the British Isles. To me she appears to be a combined manifestation of Oya, Brigit and some other energy/spirit; she is a mystery that is unique to Haiti.

For me the uncertainty around her origins is a reminder that the gods/goddesses and spirits are mysterious forces and much more than what our limited human perceptions can imagine or comprehend. While on the surface Brigit and Maman Brigitte may appear vastly different, both are associated with fertility and great powers of healing. I am also reminded that in Scottish lore Brigit is said to be two-faced, one side, the bright maiden's face of spring and life while the other side is the dark hag's face of winter and death. This dark face of Brigit, the old woman who holds the mysteries of death and transformation, is who I can see in Maman Brigitte.

Regardless of her true origins it was an especially magical experience to find that the goddess who showed up to help me deal with the ancestry I have as a result of slavery in America is possibly the same goddess who was converted to saint, transformed to Loa and today dances in a pantheon of spirits in a religion brought to Haiti by African slaves.

Breo-Saighit

My work with Brigit has led me to believe without a doubt that she is a goddess intimately connected to the lives, experiences and concerns of her children. When I call her in she shows up; her energy is strongly felt and her presence unwavering. For me the experience can sometimes feel overwhelming. Her immense power cannot be denied or dismissed. The visceral experience of her love is a force that continues to move and intrigue me. She is the sun of suns, the fiery arrow Breo-Saighit, illuminating all that is within and all that is without. She shines the light on the truth so that we may see the truth, know the truth, be the truth. Brigit keeps me in touch with the many truths, the paradox of truth. I started my work with her focusing on truths that are hard, ugly and painful. Over time, she guided me in discovering and integrating other truths, truths that hold great beauty and power.

I am a singer storyteller inspired by the poetic spirits of griots as well as bards. I am a priestess seer informed by spirits of Amengansie/Mamissiis (hereditary priestesses initiated to the African water spirit Mami Wata) and Hoodoo ladies as well as Druids, ovates and fairy doctors. I move through the world with courage, strength, pride and perseverance, supported by spirits of the Amazons of Libya and Dahomey, as well as the Celtic women warriors of the British Isles. These spirits, along with many others connected to various lands and various ancestral traditions all guide my steps and walk beside me. Carrying this truth in my heart and speaking it at times is how I've learned to honor all parts of my blood song.

With all that shared, I still cannot honestly say that I have come to an exact resolution or complete comfort when it comes to working directly with my ancestors of the Celtic lands. For me in many ways it is all still a process and I do not know exactly where it will lead me. What I do know is that I can and will forever honor and celebrate this part of who I am by continuing my relationship with and devotion to the great goddess Brigit.

References:

Filan, Kenaz. The Haitian Vodou Handbook: Protocol for Riding with the Lwa. Rochester, VT: Destiny Books, 2006.

Foubister, Laura. Goddess in the Grass: Serpentine Mythology and the Great Goddess. Toronto: EcceNova editions, 2003.

Matthews, Caitlin. The Elements of the Celtic Tradition. Dorset: Element Books, 1997.

Monoham, Patricia & McDermitt, Michael. Brigit: Sun of Womanhood. Las Vegas, NV: Goddess Ink Publications, 2013.

Monaghan, Patricia. The New Book of Goddesses and Heroines. Minneapolis, MN: Llewellyn Publications, 1997.

Stewart, R.J. Celtic Gods, Celtic Goddesses. NY: Sterling Publishing, 2006.

Tan, Mambo Chita. Haitian Vodou: An Introduction to Haiti's Indigenous Spiritual Tradition. Minneapolis, MN: Llewellyn Publications, 2012.

Acts of Love and Pleasure:
Self Nurture as a Revolutionary Art or An Introduction to the Art of Sacred Sensuality

Nadirah Adeye

This article is an "Introduction to the Art of Sacred Sensuality." My intention in writing this is to begin the process of bringing together information that I've been learning over the last 10+ years and what has been emerging from my own personal work to form the foundation of what I call Sacred Sensual Living.

I will start by offering definitions of the terms, from online dictionaries as well as my own, though readers are also welcome to incorporate their own definitions to reach their own perspective on what it means to bring the sacred and the sensual into harmony in their lives. I will continue on to explore some of the issues that illustrate the need for a shift toward a more sacred/sensual perspective in the lives of women, of women of color, of mothers (particularly during pregnancy) and of children. Finally, I will offer more information on ways that Sacred Sensual Living can address some of these issues and a couple specific practices to begin to introduce (or deepen) into the lifestyle changes offered by Sacred Sensual Living.

Sacred Sensual Living- Definitions

I've started by looking up definitions of the words Sacred and Sensual. I found that for both words (but particularly the word 'sensual') there are perceptions about the meaning that might or might not actually relate to the original definitions of the word. So I googled both words and copied the definitions from 4 or 5 different online dictionaries including Merriam-Webster, dictionary.com, Oxford Dictionaries, and MacMillan Dictionary. I've also included my own input for added clarity of what it is that *I* am referring to when I use the terms.

Sacred- connected with God (or the gods); associated with divinity or divine things; holy (meaning perceived as associated with the Divine); inspiring awe or reverence among believers; dedicated or set apart for service or worship of a deity. From the Latin *sacrum* which refers to the gods or anything in their power.

Sacred- (Nadirah's addition)- the Divine pulse that creates everything- *that* is what I am calling to when I say The Sacred- the core that prophets and seers and seekers have touched that has seeded spiritual movements and given rise to the world's various faiths.

Sensual- of or arousing gratification of the senses; pertaining to, inclined to, or preoccupied with the gratification of the senses; carnal; fleshly; relating to or affecting any of the senses or sense organs; suggesting sexuality; voluptuous. From Latin *sensus* meaning sense. It's recommended that one use the more neutral term 'sensuous' as the word sensual includes a sexual element.

Sensual- (Nadirah's addition)- We are living a human life, in human bodies. Our spirits are not defined by the body but they are certainly informed by them. I acknowledge the importance of celebrating that we are here having a sensual experience. Anyone in doubt of pleasure in our bodies as our inheritance need only take a moment and meditate on the existence of the clitoris (more on that to come). At the same time, we cannot transcend our external until we address/acknowledge what we experience and its impact.

To me, the sacred and the sensual are like the two

strands of the double helix of DNA. They are intertwined energies that swirl around us throughout our lives.

The Issues

There are several different places one can look to see the impact that modern living has on the lives and wellness of many people in the Western World. I chose to look at women's health, pregnancy and babies because of my decades-long love of pregnancy, my training as a doula, and my current phase of life- I'm doing the motherhood thing right now. Also, though, I find this a powerful place to look because even if *we* do not admit it to others or even to ourselves when we are overstressed and overburdened, even if it seems that we are getting through the days, our bodies and our babies cannot lie. They express what is happening in them and their responses with complete transparency.

In Chapter One of her book, *The Female Brain*, neuropsychiatrist Louann Brizendine, M.D. describes the ways that a baby girl "incorporates her mother's nervous system into her own" (19)

> "The nervous system environment a girl absorbs during her first two years becomes a view of the reality that will affect her for the rest of her life. Studies in mammals now show that this early stress versus calm incorporation- called epigenetic imprinting- can be passed down through several generations. Research in mammals . . . has shown that female offspring are highly affected by how calm and nurturing their mothers are. This relation has also been shown in human females and nonhuman primates. . . This isn't about what's learned cognitively- it's about what is absorbed by the cellular microcircuitry at the neurological level. . . . Neurological incorporation begins during

pregnancy. Maternal stress during pregnancy has effects on the emotional and stress hormone reactions, particularly in female offspring." (20)

Girls in utero are more susceptible than boys to their mothers' emotional states. Brizendine also states that baby girls are carrying their *own* eggs in utero- the seeds of what will become their future children. So a pregnant woman's emotional state in the NOW moment, is contributing to her granddaughter's patterns two generations from now.

According to his website, Dr. Gabor Mate' writes and speaks on "human development through the lens of science and compassion." During a presentation he gave on the "Consequences of Stressed Parenting" at the KMT Child Development & Community Conference, he states that the behaviors and issues of children [of western civilization] do not present a very encouraging picture. He talks about the importance of looking at the bio/psycho/social perspective which states that the "biology of human beings is, for a lifetime, shaped by and affected by peoples' psychological and social relationships." (Mate' online clip). He touches on a variety of health issues that we tend to consider common nowadays and says that they actually arise in children under high states of stress and are the result of the child's natural stress response being exhausted. He also states that in a society where you see stressed women, you will see stressed children. And it's quite safe to say that in the United States in 2014, many women are dealing with a significant burden of stress on a daily basis.

The documentary *Unnatural Causes* is a 7 part series that "looks at how the social, economic and physical environments in which we are born, live, and work profoundly affect our longevity and health." (unnaturalcauses.org) Part two, "When the Bough Breaks," introduces Chicago neonatologists James W. Collins Jr., MD and Richard Davis, MD who were working together to answer the question "Why do African American women have babies born too small at twice the rate of white women?" In the United States in 2002, the infant mortality rate for college educated white women was 3.7 deaths per 1,000 births. In that same year, the infant mortality rate for college educated black women was 10.2 deaths per 1,000 births. (source- Vital Statistics of the United States, 2002) Even after the doctors corrected for healthy lifestyle, education and socioeconomic status the gap remained and, in fact, widened. Babies of white women with no high school diploma had better survival rates than babies of black women with college degrees.

It was even found that African women, who arrived in the United States with infant survival rates higher than those of black American women, within two generations in the US, were displaying the rates comparable to those of African American women.

The doctors began to look at racism as a possible contributing factor. They finally reached the following conclusions:

"Racism is taking a heavy toll on African American children even before they leave their mothers' wombs." (When the Bough Breaks)

There's "something about lifelong minority status." says James W. Collins Jr., MD

"There's something about growing up as a black female in the US that's not good for your childbearing health. I don't know how else to summarize it."- Richard David, MD.

Dr. Camara Phyllis Jones, M.D. likens everyday racism to gunning the engine of a car without ever letting up. She cites a study in which the ambulatory blood pressures of black and white participants were measured during the day and at night. It was found that the white participants' blood pressures would drop in the evenings while the black participants' blood pressures remained high. As with a car, the constant "gunning" of our bodies' engines wears out the bodies themselves.

In her book Fierce Angels, Dr. Sheri Parks discusses some of the benefits and the consequences of the "Strong Black Woman" image, which is often adopted or cited as a way for African American women to handle life events that might otherwise be seen as overwhelming. "Black women have been presented with extraordinary challenges. They have had to decide whether to meet them or to turn away. Very often, they have chosen to meet them." (210) The section in which Parks discussed the health impacts of living out the Strong Black Woman ideal was of particular importance to me.

> "Dr. [Angela] Neal-Barnett conducted a study in which self-identified Strong Black Women kept diaries of their activities and emotions for a day while their blood pressures and heart rates were being monitored. She found that almost all the women were unaware of or did not admit to being stressed, even when their physical readings jumped fifteen and twenty points, indicating that their bodies were responding to stress. They told her, 'Baby, I don't have time to think about that mess. If I did, I'd be stressed out about everything.' But stress does not stop taking its toll on their bodies just because they don't acknowledge it. Refusing to acknowledge stress actually makes them more susceptible to stress-related illnesses- chronic upper-respiratory infections, hypertension, heart disease, and obesity. . . Many women take better care of their families than they do of themselves- but black women take it further." (202-203)

Dr. Michael Lu, MD, neonatologist, states that the impact of stress on health creates chronic wear and tear on the body's systems- hormonal, immune, inflammatory, and metabolic. Over time it creates an overload so they no longer function optimally. (When the Bough Breaks)

Sheri Parks (Fierce Angels) also says "stress and fatigue exact their tolls. The health problems of black women are well documented and they are often unknowingly tied to poor health care. Yet, on average, African American women take *more* preventative measures than women of any other race- more tests for high blood pressure, diabetes, more mammograms, according to the Department of Health and Human Services. Yet, they still get sick and die at higher rates." (202)

"We have to start taking care of women before pregnancy. . . when she's a baby inside her mother's womb, and an infant, and a child, and an adolescent. Really taking care of women and families across [the course of] their lives." - Michael Lu, MD, neonatologist, "When the Bough Breaks", *Unnatural Causes*.

Unnatural Causes goes on to show how doctors started incorporating meditation into prenatal care to support the mothers. They also speak about the use of meditation practices for pregnant mothers on bed rest and how it was incorporated to help them keep their babies in the womb longer, giving them crucial weeks to grow and get stronger. Even if the babies didn't make it all the way to full term, every additional day and week improved their survival rates.

So, what *is* Sacred Sensual Living?

This section is simultaneously an explanation, a prayer, a manifesto, and a casting, written on the Full Blue Moon in Aquarius.

Before continuing, let's pause. Take a moment to inhale deeply, filling your lungs and rounding your belly. Exhale (releasing an "Ahhh" or a "Hmmmmm" if you feel comfortable doing so). Send your roots down into the Earth, reaching as deeply as you can, and begin drawing

Earth energy up and into your core. Send your awareness up and out toward the moon, connecting with Her and begin drawing lunar energy down into your core. Allow the two energies to mingle, inhaling and exhaling deeply. Then allow them to flow upward into your heart and out to your arms, and down into your pelvic cradle, and out into your legs and feet. Feel your entire self being filled with these mingled Earth and Lunar energies. (Feel free to send more into places that may need some added nourishment in the moment.) Then allow Earth to return to Earth and Moon to return to Moon. Take one more deep breath, release and continue reading.

I realized, about 5 years ago, through a series of personal meditations that took place over the course of a year and a half, that one of the most important things we can do as spiritual practitioners, is to find an internal state of harmony and alignment and bring that out into the world around us- to speak, act and move from that state. Francesca Gentille, in her Sacred Courtesan Trainings, teaches that we (as healers, spiritual beings, teachers, etc.) need to align ourselves heart, mind, body, spirit *and* Eros as we do our work.

One of my favorite books is *The Kin of Ata Are Waiting for You* by Dorothy Bryant. In the story, the culture of the kin is all about remaining in alignment so that they can be in harmony with the sacred pursuits of the collective. They have womb-like structures that anyone can enter any time they are in need of healing whether it's physical or mental or emotional re-centering.

I have noticed, in our society and even in myself, that there is a way in which growth through suffering is applauded, working to exhaustion, pushing ourselves to our limits and beyond. I live my life in this way- pushing my limits so that every year I can look back and see that I have grown in certain ways. Stepping out of this pattern is something I continue to work on shifting, but what I am advocating for (particularly for women and especially for those who are mothering or working in fields that involve nurturing others) is a recognition that for our own health and vitality, as well as for the continuity of whatever individual missions we are here to fulfill, *it is crucial that we expand our capacity for pleasure in equal measure to our capacity to face suffering*. It must be non-negotiable that we make time and space to realign, to nourish ourselves and to dive into pleasure- whatever that means for us.

Racism/sexism/homophobia/injustice are not going away any time soon. Neither is the fact that adulthood, relationships, parenting and ambition about our own lives and goals will require that we deal with stress. Sacred Sensual Living is about the importance of how we deal with these situations, knowing that they are currently a part of our collective reality. I also envision it as a way for us to connect with others so that we can be encouraged and kept accountable for our commitments to nurture ourselves.

Where do you find peace? Serenity? Balance? It can be something as deep as the altered states one can access through ritual and sacred practices like chanting but it can also be things that seem "shallow." When I was a teenager (with significantly fewer responsibilities and much more time), I loved to pamper myself. I spent hours on things like facials, conditioning my hair, doing my nails, massage and reading about new ways to do all of the above. There were a few times when I spent almost an hour just applying my lipstick perfectly, even though I had no place to go. What I enjoyed most about those experiences was the access to (what I now know were) meditative states. They were moments of stillness, focus, pleasure and receptivity merging together as a result of something I was doing.

Sacred Sensual Living arises from that love of pampering and self-nurturing. Even with the responsibilities of life and the challenges of adulthood, there are still gateways to those feelings of harmony and spaciousness, pleasure and peace to be found in moments of self-care.

Pleasure is our birthright. Heads up- this is the clitoris part I said was coming up. We, who are female born, are blessed with the clitoris, a structure that serves no purpose but pleasure and contains about 8,000-9,000 nerve endings (for comparison, the penis has about 4,000 nerve endings). Here is a quote from the Museum of Sex blog "Consider this: In over five million years of human evolution, only one organ has come to exist for the sole purpose of providing pleasure – the clitoris. It is not required for reproduction . . . Its sole function – its singular, wonderful purpose – is to make a woman feel good!!" (You are welcome to take a moment and re-read that several more times.)

As Regina Thomashaur, also known as Mama Gena, stated in her TED talk *The Pleasure Revolution* "You have 8,000 nerve endings dedicated to pleasure. If 8,000 of your thoughts every day are not about pleasure, 8,000 of your dreams, and 8,000 of your desires, then you are not living the design of what it means to be a woman."

Sacred Sensual Living is also, to me, about the importance of Sanctuary. Women of color, in particular, need a place (in the world and inside of themselves) that is a sanctuary from the outside world. We need recharge time. We need nurturing and to step into our own capacities to receive. In order to receive, we must be able to leave space for another to fill it and when a life is full of stress (financial, career, relationships, racism and other prejudices, health, etc.) and we live in perpetual *doing*, everything has a schedule. Spaciousness takes time, yes, but leaving space for someone else to support us can throw off an entire schedule and feel like a threat to our survival.

Sacred Sensual Living is for everyone who feels

connected to the path, but I am especially motivated by the need for African American women to have time and space for a break, for some peace, to recharge.

As I have been moving forward on this path of Sacred Sensuality, I have realized over and over that, with the state of our world today, it is a revolutionary act for a woman to treat herself with kindness, to be gentle with herself, to honor her need for harmony and sanctuary.

Here is the definition of the word revolution-

> A radical and pervasive change in society and the social structure, a sudden, complete or marked change in something; a sudden, radical or complete change; a fundamental change in the way of thinking about or visualizing something; a change of paradigm; a dramatic and wide-reaching change in the way something works or is organized or in people's ideas about it. (Oxford, MacMillan, Merriam-Webster online)

The history of women, of women of color, of African American women, in this nation and on this planet is full of harsh trials and overcoming obstacles. It is time that we treat our need for tenderness as sacred, time that we embrace the idea that to treat ourselves gently is a way of honoring the gods, time that we establish harmonious alignment between heart, mind, body and spirit as a non-negotiable priority and acknowledge the fact that when we are there- we have the capacity to do our greater work in the world, to be effective in our lives, to face down and resist injustice, to create a different world/society that works for all of its' inhabitants rather than a select privileged few.

As it has been stated, so may it be. Amina.

Exercises

1. Cultivate a practice (or practices) that connects you directly to the Divine. If you already know what they are, seek out more, increase the frequency you are doing them, or increase the amount of time you devote to them.

2. Cultivate a practice (or practices) that connects you to beauty/joy/pleasure in your body, in your home, in the world around you. Study your own relationship to the sensual world. If you've already started, take it to the next level by adding additional practices, or do something that you know would make you feel wonderful, but you've put off doing until now. Make a list of things you would *love* to do (though you might currently have restrictions of finances, time, or access).

Conclusion

Our bodies and our babies are revealing the unhealthy patterns of our society. They are speaking to the madness of what we have come to accept as normal.

Sacred Sensual Living is about the importance of living in alignment, of balance. It's as simple as that. The act of treating ourselves with kindness and tenderness is revolutionary, it's a contribution to the "pain to pleasure shift" that is taking place according to Riane Eisler in the book *Sacred Pleasure*. It's about the radical, revolutionary act of saying "I deserve to feel good in my skin. I am no longer willing to NOT feel as good as it's possible to feel in this skin, and this body."

Sacred Sensual Living is about the art of living from and within your own sweet spot.

The mission of Sacred Sensual Living is to create a life that honors the sacred, celebrates the sensual, and to live a life that is sustainable for self and the Earth.

Resources

Brizendine, Louann. *The Female Brain.* New York: Broadway Books, 2006. Print
Bryant, Dorothy. *The Kin of Ata are Waiting for You.* Berkeley: Moon Books, 1971. Print.
Dictionary.com. Web. August 2013.
Eisler, Riane. *Sacred Pleasure: Sex, Myth, and the Politics of the Body--New Paths to Power and Love.* San Francisco: HarperSanFrancisco, 1995. Print.
Gentille, Francesca. *The Sacred Courtesan School.* Web. August 2013.
MacMillan Dictionary. Web. August 2013.
Mate', Gabor. "Consequences of Stressed Parenting." *KMT Child Development & Community Conference April 2012.* Toronto: TVO Parents. May 2012. YouTube.
Mate', Gabor. *Dr. Gabor Mate'.* Web. August 2013.
Melodiousmsm. "The Internal Clitoris." *Museum of Sex Blog.* Web. August 2013.
Merriam-Webster. Web. August 2013.
Oxford Dictionaries. Web. August 2013.
Parks, Sheri. *Fierce Angels: Living with a Legacy from the Sacred Dark Feminine to the Strong Black Woman.* Chicago: Chicago Review Press, Inc. 2013. Print.
Thomashauer, Regena. "The Pleasure Revolution." *TEDxFiDiWomen.* Repretoireproductions.com. December 2011. YouTube.
"When the Bough Breaks." Unnatural Causes: Is Inequality Making Us Sick?. California Newsreel with Vital Pictures, 2008. Film.

Paganism and the Path Back to Africa

Yvonne E. Nieves

I am about to celebrate my third complete year as a self-initiated Pagan Witch. Four years ago an orisha came to me in a dream, beaconing me to the path of witchcraft for she, Oya, is the mother of all Witches. Shortly after Oya's appearance to me, I decided to commit a complete year and a day to establishing for myself a foundation of witchcraft that I would be able to build upon for the remainder of my days. I celebrated every Wiccan holiday, every Sabbath and Esbat with my own rituals and celebrations honoring the change in season and nature's energies within me.

This solitary year and a day allowed me the space to make my own informed decisions about what it means to be a person of true spiritual conviction. It taught me self-discipline, how to meditate, and how to not be afraid. Many energies came to me during this time including Celtic goddesses, Mayan ancestors and Scandinavian deities. However, from the very first day, I committed to having a permanent altar to Elegua, the African orisha whom must be recognized first before any others are connected with, as well as Oya, the goddess of my dream.

To me, it was very important that I consistently honor these two particular energies. Elegua assisted in opening the roads for me, and supported every new venture of my life, including obtaining a new job. Oya's energies were strong, as she rules over the cemetery and is herself the wind of change. Who knew that Oya's presence in my life during my first year would bring about so many shifts, which corrected, and rightly directed my path? She was so very loving, but very direct, often times blowing things up in my face –literally. I had an offering cup of coffee explode on me, but not hurt me, in order to signal that I was making a drastically wrong decision in my life. Oya kept me in check and even moved me around - literally to different apartments in my Pilsen, Chicago neighborhood- until I finally settle into a place that would allow me the safety and space to work on my shadow self, receive greater incite and develop my spiritual gifts.

My worship with the two orishas was consistent. Elegua was given fresh water every Monday, and he had his candy, cigars and rum to keep him appeased while he guards my front door. Oya also had a permanent space in my apartments during this time of change; she was always housed close to my witchy books and my *vejigante* masks from Puerto Rico. Both would patiently observe my magickal workings and correct me when things needed to be corrected, and both would not mind if I worked with others outside of the African pantheon. To me, this was paganism – eclectically immersing myself with various pre-Judeo-Christian pantheons, engaging myself in related theoretical studies of religion and becoming familiar with the god and goddess aspects within myself.

This time, however, was a bit frustrating, as I so wanted to connect with Elegua and Oya on deeper levels. I identified with Oya so much so that I hoped I was her daughter. In traditional Wiccan practices it is perfectly acceptable to select a deity –or allow for a deity select you- as their child, and thus establish a life-long spiritual relationship with the deity. However, I knew that this perhaps would not be the case for me with Oya. I knew that she came to me initially, but that she could have simply lead me to this new way of living life in spirit. At the time I felt that the only way to get deeper into working with these two Orishas was to work in Santeria. Santeria did not draw me, especially because all that I had known about Santeria was the religious syncretism that had occurred through Catholicism and the replacement of African orishas into saints. I did not want to worship Catholic saints. I wanted to work with the energy and essence of my mother Africa that was free of colonial influences and in its purest form.

In April 2013 I found myself at the threshold of consciously committing myself to working with the orishas for the rest of my life, including my mother Yemaya, Oya's sister who is the goddess of the sea and mother of all orishas, who revealed herself to me in a previous divination ceremony conducted with five *babalawos*, or priests of Ifa. I had decided to remain Pagan, but more seriously delve into working with the energies from Africa that had followed me here, to this time and space. My initiation into Ifa, the system of divination said to be over 8,000 years old (according to author Ayo Salami) that helps guide all humans in every aspect of their lives –including what to eat and when to see a doctor, for example- would be a way that I could both pay homage and work to heal my African ancestors. Elegua and Oya had done such a great job supporting me up until that moment that I couldn't deny Olodumare's -or God's- dominion any longer.

I entered into a three day ceremony in order to become an *apetebi*, or wife of Orula, the orisha who rules over Ifa, and assume responsibilities of carrying for my warriors (orishas that one is initiated into during this primary ceremony), learning about the varying paths associated with Ifa and West Africa, as well as serving my godfathers and fellow god brothers and sisters of in my *ile*, or spiritual house. Aspects of the ceremony are kept secret, and the initiate is expected to enter into the sacred space with perfect love and perfect trust – a religious value taught in Wicca and other spiritual paths- for his or her godfathers and the *ile* family.

What a grand time it was, albeit personally

challenging at moments, but my commitment to working within the West African pantheon was solidified. My relationships to the orishas were strengthened. The power I felt within me and the strength of the spirits I encountered made me appreciate my path on much deeper levels. The information that has been revealed to me since my ceremony has confirmed my overall commitment to Paganism. And whether or not I commit myself deeper into the Yoruban religious path or ever physically travel to Africa on this dimension or in this lifetime, I know that I have fulfilled a great responsibility to my ancestors from the motherland. I have learned that I am my ancestors, and they are me. In as such, I have given myself the gift of understanding the power that I retain within my own divine genetic structure, and am working toward healing trans-generational wounds stemming from the loss of language, culture, religion and historic memory, which occurred during the trans-Atlantic slave trade. By intentionally connecting with and healing them through time and space, I connect and heal myself. Ache!

On Those Whose Shoulders We Stand

Luna Pantera

I'm use to going to a Pagan gathering and having the question come up, *"Why do we need to invoke ancestors when casting a circle?"* I used to be surprised, but now I'm just very disappointed. Can a tree stand in a harsh storm with wind and rain unless it has strong roots? A majority of culture's Ancestor reverence is as common a practice as birth, rites of adulthood, weddings/handfasts, or celebration of transition of life/funerals. Pagans always say, "What is remembered lives" when a love one passes over. Do we say these words without really understand the full meaning behind them?

Ancestor reverence became very meaningful for me at a time when I was in deep turmoil and feeling very alone. I was going through an intense custody battle with my soon to be ex-husband. My family had literally turned their backs on me, as they did not believe in divorce per se. I had recently inherited my great grandmother's several times over ring by chance. I had awoken up in the middle of the night from a nightmare that had escaped me. I was left with the feeling of absolute hopelessness and feeling totally alone. I had been told by my mother, who had given me the ring, that the previous owner had been a voodoo woman out of Louisiana and had been the protector of the family. No one messed with her or hers when she lived. Wearing the ring gave me a feeling of safety, and while still new to the craft I wasn't sure how much was "real" and how much was useful thinking. I sat up in bed, closed my eyes, and allowed all the emotions I was feeling come to the surface. I begged her to show me that she was real, that I was not alone, and that she would help me through whatever it was I needed to go through. The apartment was completely empty as my daughter had the week with her father. I had no pets at the time. I felt someone/something sit on my bed and grab my foot and gently squeeze it to let me know, "all was well." Now, being a recovering Catholic at the time raised on horror movies, I politely thanked her for her presence and requested that she leave for the time being as I was about to have major heart failure!

My Ancestor reverence was cemented after 9/11. The night of 9/11 the spiritual community I was a part of at the time had a gathering for us to do some spiritual work for those who had passed over. There was a trance, and from the trance I got very strongly that now was the time to work with both our Ancestors and the Fey/Earth Spirits to help with the coming that had already been occurring and that was only going to intensify.

I know for a fact that most of my magik is from the past lives I have lived and from the DNA that runs in my blood. I am constantly coming across clients who are magikal and in fact I can "sense" their Ancestors beside them waiting for them to contact them. They're waiting to share the knowledge, wisdom, strength and courage that are part of their linage.

I always tell my clients and students that the best teacher to help you to remember the magik that resides within you is to find an Ancestor that is willing to take you on as their apprentice. I believe that as we are elevated we elevate them, and they really do have our best interest at heart. That doesn't mean that we take on all comers! If you were having a party in your home, do you leave the door open and place a sign that states all Are Welcome? I think not! The same goes when "screening" potential Spirit Guides/Ancestors. It helps if you know a little about them beforehand. If not, you can ask.

I know that in my family tree there is a deep wound

that goes all the way down to the roots, and I have been the one "tasked" with helping to heal that wound. The only way that I can do this is to work with "those that came before me" to see where it all started and to work with them to heal that original wound and to allow that healing to reverberate to heal us in the here and now!

I have written a play using the potent words of Beah Richards, (who I see as an artistic Ancestor) from her powerful monologue, "A Black Woman Speaks." I have taken her piece and broken it down into several parts: Beah Richards herself, The African Ancestor, The Slave, The Higher Consciousness of White Women, and the Descendant. The actress/priestess in the play work with both the energy of the Ancestor they are invoking and the Orisha that calls to work with them. The play is powerful because it invokes truth in the current relationships between Black and White women by explaining the history that is between us, and how it still affects us to this day.

I will not work with anyone magikal if they cannot call in their Ancestors. If you don't feel comfortable calling them in, you haven't looked back far enough. No one's entire family tree was always slave owners, racist, or criminals. Everyone has the wise man or woman who knew the herbs, had the magik, and loves his or her family more than themselves. And if you can't find them easily, perhaps you need to start a little understanding/forgiving/healing to get to them!

With that said, I would like to offer those interested in starting to work with their Ancestors a little ritual that you can use and add to it you as you see fit to open the door of working with your Ancestors.

Ritual for Working with Your Ancestors

It is important to figure out how you would like to begin to work with your Ancestors. Do you feel there is healing that needs to be done, or would you like to just open up a door of communication? Use your intuition of what phase of the moon would be right for you.

Tools you will need

A mirror, preferably white, that will only be used for this work. The mirror should stay covered up and/or put away when not in use.

Dried pink rose petals or buds (organic if possible)
Rose oil (essential oil is preferably)
Lavender oil (essential oil is preferably)
Salt (preferably course sea salt)

Two white candles (tea lights or votive candles would do fine) and a candle that will be used to invoke working with your Ancestors.

A bowl to consecrate your rose petals. (I would suggest a white one)

A place to set up your altar, which will include: a white plate that will only be used to "feed" the Ancestors, a white tea cup (if you know them to have been tea or coffee drinkers, a glass to pour them libations of a "stronger nature", and a white goblet that will be filled with spring water that is to be changed once a week, a candle that will represent the covenant you are making to your Ancestors and an Ancestor stone. You can choose your altar cloth to be a color you feel drawn to, white for purity and spirit, purple for Ancestor wisdom and magik, pink/blue for healing, green for love, etc…

A light colored garment to put on after the bath. (white is preferred)

The Ritual

I would suggest you set up your altar first. Please feel free to refer to "Jambalaya" by Luisha Teish for instruction.

Next take your white bowl and fill it with your rose petals/buds and leave it on your altar for a full moon cycle. Ask that the Deities of the Ancestors of whatever path you walk, to bless and prepare the roses for the work you will do.

Once the rose petals have been consecrated you can begin your work. Samhain would be ideal, and if that is too long to wait imagine you are "greasing the wheel" for the powerful work.

First you will prepare your bath salt by mixing two cup of salt with a quarter cup of rose petals and nine drops of rose and lavender oil. You will keep what you don't use in a consecrated container.

Cast a circle to include both your Ancestor altar and your bathtub. Call in your Deities and guides to assistant you in this work.

Light your candle and welcome those Ancestors who are willing to work with you for the highest good of both yourself and your bloodline.

Draw your bath and throw in three small handfuls of bath salt, imagine that this bath is purify you of any fears or doubts you may have and opening the door to work with your Ancestors.

When the bath is ready, bring your candle into the bathroom and set it close by to call about your guides, to cleanse and prepare you to meet the Spirits of your blood.

Once out, dress in your white garment, go back to your altar. Take out your mirror and smudge it with sage and rub it with the bath salts to consecrate it, and ask the spirit of the mirror to show you what you are ready to see. Wipe the mirror of any excess oil or salt, and then place the mirror on your altar. Turn out all other lights and light the two white candles, and place them on either side of the mirror. Allow your mind to soften and ask that the Ancestor who will be your gatekeeper to reveal his or herself to you in the mirror. If you do not see a vision but one forms in your head...allow it to shape, see if you can get a name. See if they have a gift for you to form this covenant/partnership. Offer them a gift to seal the deal. Remind them that this is a partnership of love and light, and will remain so. If you feel comfortable, invite them into your dreams to continue the discussion.

Once you are back, journal your experience. And if you did not have a conscience contact the first time, don't give up. See if you can find something you could offer them on your altar that might entice them. Remember that the white plate and cup is to be used only for their offerings and should always be washed and re-consecrated with salt after every use.

Working with Ancestors can opening up worlds that you had no idea existed. They can give you inside information to your family dynamics, allow you to learn more about your magikal lineage, and more importantly, have an ally on the other side that can help filter out spirits that you choose to work with. Ancestors are there to help, education, protect and guide us, especially in these changing times. Open to them and you will be rewarded.

Ashe!

Finding Divinity in the Deep South

Nathaniel Puckett

Nestled in the Appalachian foothills of North Georgia, cradled in Oak, Poplar and Pine, you'll find a small city where I spent the vast majority of my childhood. Though most of my memories are pleasant, there is still an underlying undulating fear of the place I used to call home. You see I don't fit in to the "general" demographic of Jasper, Ga. In a Bible Belt City of 3,684 where 93% of the population is white, a multiracial, bi sexual, Pagan, male is something most people can't understand, won't tolerate. If I was fortunate, most people shied away from me. However, the emotional and physical scars I bear testify, that all too often, I wasn't so lucky.

What little solace there was to find was had in a small batch of pine and poplar tucked behind an old, powder blue and white-stained-brown, two room trailer that I called home; the woods not the trailer. The woods were small and thin, barely even dense enough to be considered a thicket, much less the "forest" my child mind believed. The days I spent in that little batch of trees, nestled into a bed of pine needles and poplar leaves are far too numerous to count. I had found my sanctuary, and the bigotry and racism couldn't reach me there. I was safe in that little copse to be who I really was, to live my own life and not the one that was expected of me. It was in that little grove that my feet first found my sacred path.

Prayer was never something that came easy to me. The one room Southern Baptist church that occupied so much of my childhood held a special pain for me. I was a subject of discussion or seen as a curiosity, at best, a malady at worst. But as in all things, some good came of this. The cold hard looks of the people who waited behind those old double doors taught me the first truth I ever learned. The eyes won't lie. While their lips would smile and fill the air with pretty little pleasantries, their eyes would betray their nature. I could read their thoughts through their eyes as easily as a news anchor reading a teleprompter, and I would suffer under their scrutiny, wearing the color of my skin with shame.

Time seemed to crawl in that little wood box of a church. The hymns and prayers seemed to last an eternity and I was certain I'd be an old man by the time everyone had finished their prayer requests. The day would drag on and on but eventually the sermons always ended the same. With a red faced and winded preacher standing amongst the congregation, brow heavy with sweat as his threats of damnation hung in the air, I found my sense of peace. Not due to any touch of divinity but simply because it was over. The preacher was exhausted with yelling and that meant that we could go home now; my grandmother to her shows, my mother to her books and me to my woods.

Without fail, rain or shine, I would find myself in those woods. All that I required was the sanctity of those trees. Their old familiar faces would watch silently as I played my little games, or dozed at their feet, or in the outstretched arms that were their branches. I would sing to them and the sigh of the wind through their leaves would speak their approval. I was perfectly content in those moments, sitting and listening to the songs and stories of the woods. The crow and whippoorwill would sing with me and carry on conversations into the night where their stories would be taken up by the katydids and crickets. Even in the late hours long after I was supposed to be asleep, I would find myself by my window listening to the wood songs and dreaming happily.

As the years passed, and I grew older, an amazing

thing occurred. A library opened. In the same city I lived in. Now this may not seem like a big deal to most but for someone who was reading on a college level by the time I hit high school, this was a profound occasion. As a result, more and more time was spent with my face buried in between the covers of a wide and varying range of literature. I was reading everything, from fantasy and sci-fi to autobiographies and historical fiction. To put it simply, if it had words I was reading them. This sudden flood of accessibility paved the way for a subject matter I had never placed any thought into: theology. I began to devour book after book on the religions of the world (what small selection my backwoods library provided), Buddhism, Shinto, Taoist philosophy and Hinduism, from the Quran and the Torah, to books on shamanism and Native American Spirituality. I filled my life with beliefs and faiths from across the globe, finally stumbling upon an old tattered copy of a book on modern paganism and Wicca.

To this day I cannot recall the name of the book or who even wrote it. Ironically many of the concepts were ridiculous to me. However, there was one thing that caught my attention enough to start a spark and that was speaking to nature. My world shook and as I sat in a dark corner of my little library, curled around a book that most of my community would consider Satanic, I realized that I was not alone. Out there somewhere lost amongst the masses was someone who believed the same as I. Someone who sang their songs for the trees, and listened, and rejoiced as the world returned the song. I was elated, ecstatic and positively beside myself with joy. I wasn't weird. Too terrified to bring the book into my house, I hid it away in a tiny crevice of shelving at the library, where I prayed no one would find it. I headed home to my woods to speak to my old friends of the joy I had discovered and what happened next I will never forget.

That night, under the darkness of a new moon, (the

importance of which was entirely lost on me at the time), I snuck out of my bedroom window and slipped into the woods behind the old trailer. I sat with my friends, sang and spoke with them in hushed whispers with fear of being discovered. Without knowing the weight of my words or the influence they would have on my future, I sang a song to the trees and the earth. I sang of loyalty and respect, of honor and commitment. I pledged myself to the forest in song and spirit, and in that moment nothing else mattered. I was only thirteen as I sat amongst those trees but the second truth of my life was revealed to me that night. I was sacred. I was one with the trees and the forest. I was just as much a part of them as they were with me. One being, a single entity spread amongst countless vessels. We were divine.

 I cried that night and I cry still when I think back to a scrawny little kid in cutoff shorts alone in the woods on a warm night in the middle of a Georgia Summer, rejoicing in the divinity of nature and sacredness of self. I was no longer my mocha skin or my father's bastard son. I was no longer my curly black hair or my almond brown eyes. I was beyond things like facial features, or bone structure, or a big backside. I was every tree, every leaf, and every animal that crawled in the dirt or flew in the sky. I was the forest that I had so dearly loved and I have never looked back.

 Years later I find myself living with a Priestess who leads a small eclectic pagan community and again I am the minority. I fully understand that in the eyes of most I am a bit of an anomaly, a multiracial male in a very Eurocentric world of feminine divinity. It was not until very recently however, that I gave much thought to this. While trying to put together an Esbat Ritual, my Priestess provides me with a book on the meanings of full moons and their associated Gods/Goddesses, yet we notice something odd. The European and Hindu pantheons were there in full force. The Greek and Roman Divinities we all know more or less about had their standard seats at the forefront of each chapter, there are even instances of Japanese and Egyptian spirituality, and yet there was an obvious lack of African Divinity. This spurs my Priestess into a series of questions (as she is apt to do). Have I ever noticed this before? What forms of divinity have I personally felt drawn to? Does the book's lack of African Divinity bother me? All of these questions swim around inside my mind tugging at strings and long buried emotions, and finally produce a ground breaking and awe inspiring answer, "I don't know." Was that all I had? I knew there had to be more to it than that and I began to evaluate how the situation could bring about such indifference.

I start the process of picking at my own psyche and eventually come to the root of the issue, my father, or rather the lack of my father's role in my life. My mother is almost fully Irish and I pull my African and American Indian ancestry from my biological father, whom my mother had left while I was still very young. At my Grandmother's insistence I had studied Native American and African American civil rights issues but there had never been a spur to delve deeper into my African roots. I knew my ancestry had come from slavery. I knew that at some point the descendant of a freed slave had married a young Cherokee woman and from them my Great Grandfather was born, but that summed up all I knew of my father's lineage. Africa had never been a part of my life so I had never felt drawn to its divinity. I further discovered that I was not surprised by this. I have always had a rooting in Celtic spirituality, and more often than not, found myself drawn to the Celtic or Nordic Pantheons. Upon this realization something truly thought provoking hit me. "I guess it is what I have come to expect. It is hard to notice what isn't there and easier to accept something because it is what you have come to expect to be there." This has become my final answer for my Priestess and it shakes my soul.

A feeling long forgotten begins to crawl its way up inside me, digging at the pit of my stomach. A feeling I had tried to leave in my past and yet continually seems to find its way back into my life. This time however I was on the other end and I was terrified. Had I somehow done a disservice to myself by ignoring my African roots? Was I in some way being inadvertently bigoted toward that part of my ancestry? If so, was it out of some buried disdain for my biological father? I struggle with this clash of new and old emotions, and decide I have some very serious soul searching ahead of me.

As I meditate on these new revelations and try to sort my way through all the confusion, I realize something important. I had subconsciously adopted an "out of sight, out of mind" attitude toward my African lineage which was not, in and of itself, wrong. However, my desire to love and understand all things had not included my African heredity. Passively ignoring and filing away my roots had served to counteract the core of my philosophies; "All divinity are one and we are one with all divinity." Armed with this new understanding of self I realized that there is need for me to study things of Africa in order to find and tap into that divine nature, and that learning these things will reaffirm my belief that anyone can feel a connection to divinity of any culture. In sharing our culture and beliefs, we better ourselves and our community. We may even begin seeing those African mysteries in Esbats and Sabbats books in the future. Even as I struggle with better understanding my heritage, my heart will always belong to a small grove of Poplar and Pine in the North Georgia foothills where a scrawny kid in cut off shorts first heard divinity speak the words he would repeat as a mantra for the rest of his life. You are loved and you are Divine.

I am Irish. I am Cherokee. I am African. I am Pagan. I am Bi Sexual.
I am loved.
I am Divine.

Stereotypes, Prejudice, and the Impact on Spiritual or Magickical Workings

Jayde Van Ter Pool

"Truth is the currency of love" (Wright).
   This adage I find profound and poignant. Truth has been an integral part in all of the religions that I've followed, whether organized or not. This is my journey and my truth. My name is Jayde and I am a Witch. My hope for you is that on your journey of discovery you find all of what you seek spiritually. Ashe)0(
   Family members always told me that I come from a long line of those who "practice". The word practice I distinctly remember being used intermittently along with its true name; Witchcraft.
   I can recall being told stories of my ancestors who were from a tiny island in the Caribbean. One of which was a distant cousin who delivered all of the babies of the village. She delivered my Grandmother, Mother, my Aunts and Uncles as well. She was a shaman who helped heal ailments using ritual and incorporating powerful herbs. It was no hidden secret within the family that she used Voodoo for healing. To this day her memory is still highly respected by the villagers from the tiny island.
   Although it was mostly the women in my family that practiced Voodoo, there was one male ancestor that was a very powerful practitioner. He was, and still is, revered by many in the community and has become folklore.
   I am eclectic racially. I am eclectic spiritually. I descend from African-Caribbean, German, Scottish, and

Chinese roots, with a European upbringing. I embrace all types of Magick, although my earliest memories are from my African-Caribbean roots and Voodoo. I incorporate my rituals today based on a wide range of teachings, but am sincerely exultant at where my journey with Witchcraft began.

As far back as I can remember Witchcraft has always had a place in the household during my childhood and continues to today. Growing up, stories of my lineage were shared with me and my siblings, but it was I that had been chosen by my ancestors to continue in their footsteps. I became "The Keeper". I am the Keeper of mysteries. My role was to take part in the performance of rituals and spells, and also to keep a record of both, written and by memory. This was to be my part and purpose in life within the family.

A fond memory from my childhood was being allowed to attend, what I call now, the gathering of Magickal women. These were female friends and family members who would purposely allow me to sit with them during their "grown up" conversations. I loved attending these and somehow knew this was part of my role. I was allowed to hear grown up stuff which I found to be a bonus.

Meetings were private and behind closed doors. My siblings were allowed to go out and play and enjoyed being children. They never asked me what was discussed and seemed as if they had no interest. I, on the other hand, grew up quickly listening to all of the adult affairs. As a result of my attendance, the women began to include me in discussion and ritual. Soon they began asking for my advice, particularly when there was an issue where they could find no resolution.

It was at these Magical gatherings that I felt the strong, powerful energies of the Witches and Voodoo Priestess' and will never forget it. From time to time I will feel that same type of energy when I am in the presence of a large group of Pagans, especially females. It is a feeling like no other.

The discussions were primarily about daily life within the community. Back then I felt all of this to be mundane, but now I understand that all the topics discussed were of great importance because we were healing, and addressing community concerns with the power of Magick. Soon I realized that in all topics of conversation Magick always played an integral part.

I enjoyed the rituals after meetings most of the time because I was able to take part at such a young age. Other times I did not enjoy myself, and wished that I could just go outside with my siblings and play. Looking back I can understand and appreciate that it was all a part of my journey of becoming a Witch. Some might say I was being groomed, and that I didn't really have a choice, but I know this not to be the case, for there are things that I saw, heard and was privy to well before I knew what Witchcraft was.

Witchcraft was alive in all aspects of my daily life even with something as simple as cooking a meal. There is a recipe I was taught for fish which had to be prepared and cooked using ritual before being consumed. There is a belief that eating certain parts of the animal could make you stronger and protect you from those that would do you harm. Needless to say, due to our beliefs, the food thing meant that we ate a strict diet, and were never allowed to take food from people we didn't know. That meant no junk food and no restaurants.

Even when we groomed our hair, Witchcraft was involved. We would be preparing our hair to be put in "cane rows", and any loose hair from grooming would need to be burned. The belief is that the hair contained our energy, and if in the hands of someone else they could use it against us or control every aspect of our being for their gain.

We lived our lives our way, with a reverence for Magick and an affinity for nature. I loved the way we lived and I still live this way today. Even though my siblings were not privy to the gatherings, we still shared the same spirituality and they also took part in ritual. It didn't occur to me that we were looked at as different until I started school and realized that other families were not like mine.

To everyone outside of the family we were practicing Catholics. So not only were we Witches, but we practiced Catholicism at the same time. There is such a contradiction between the two, that at times it was confusing. I remember feeling unrestricted with Witchcraft and the God/dess, and I had a sense of freeness. While on the other hand, I felt restricted practicing Catholicism. I can remember feeling this way from a young age. We knew that being different would mean being stereotyped and then subsequently ridiculed by our community, even though I knew of other families who were also 'practicing'. So we hid what we truly believed in, and learned from a very young age to just keep it secret.

But like oil rising to the top of water, our 'secret' eventually got out into the community in the form of neighborhood gossip. In the Caribbean, especially the small islands, everybody knows everybody else's business. The same mentality found its way across the waters to Europe with the Caribbean communities. Gossip spread about the lineage of my family, and that we may have dabbled in Voodoo. Although it could never be substantiated, the stigma was there. People who had previously talked to us suddenly stopped. We were teased by the children at school, and my older sister and I were bullied. In addition we were ignored by the adults in the community.

I didn't like my Sunday school teacher, and I kept getting into trouble. I kept reading the "holy book" and questioning it. The questions I asked would anger the teacher and she would complain to my Mum. Knowing that I was just trying to make sense of what the truth was, between Witchcraft and what they were teaching at Sunday school, my Mother really had no response to the teachers' complaints.

Growing up in a household like mine with a secret wasn't easy. I was now exposed to something other than the Catholic Church, which meant that I was now thinking outside of the box. There was still so much that I wanted to know. I recall reading the children's version of the bible. It taught that Jesus rose from the dead to visit his disciples and his Mother, but when I mentioned that I was visited by family who were no longer here I was severely reprimanded. I was confused. I was reminded that only Jesus could rise from the dead and visit those he loved and give a message. Before long I was kicked out. I was supposed to be a lamb and follow the shepherd named Jesus. I laugh about it now, but back then I was confused and nobody explained anything to me.

I did not like church. I didn't like the other kids and they teased me because I seemed different. I looked at the world differently, not through a child's eye. I didn't play like the other kids. I saw things that they couldn't see. I also didn't think like a child because of my attendance at the gatherings.

I loved to go out alone and spend most of my day and night in nature. This is where I felt welcomed and at peace. I would fall asleep in the branches of a large oak tree, or lie in the tall grass and wait to hear voices, the whispers of nature, and the voices of my ancestors amongst all the other sounds. I would eat blackberries off the vine, and pull rhubarb from the soil to take home to bake rhubarb crumble. The other kids liked nature because of the wide-open spaces where they could play football, kiss-chase, and other childhood games. Looking back I can see why they teased me. I was just in a different space.

Growing up, I think what affected me negatively the most was not the kids making fun of me, but the adult's non acceptance of myself, and my siblings. They judged us even though we were the same as them.

I am nine years old when my Aunt came to live with us. I love my aunt and she is what I can only describe as "free spirited". She is acutely aware of my gifts and encourages me to enhance them. It is during my Aunt's stay that I accompanied her to a community hall where I was introduced to her spiritual partner. He seemed to me to be at least eight feet tall with locks that reached down to the base of his back. To me he resembled Bob Marley. This was the day that I was introduced to Rastafari.

The cadenced, hypnotic, uninterrupted sounds of African drums, this is Nyabinghi. The hands of the community elders, mostly men, pounded out the rhythms as chanting fills the room along with the "Holy Herb". The smoke and simultaneous chanting with the rhythm of the drum, lifts the room from this dimension to the next. You know when the ancestors arrive, their presence was strong. I can remember the ancestors showing their attendance via the heavy smoke that saturated the room. I could clearly see human forms being taken on with the use of the smoke from the sacred herb. This is how we, "I and I", communicated with our ancestors. 'I and I' was used frequently in our daily dialogue and via scripture, and I loved its meaning. It simply meant 'You' and 'Me', and it also meant that all are equal in the eyes of Jah Rastafari. Nyabinghi was what I deemed at the time as the replacement of "Church", was amazing.

The elders would quote from the Bible, but in a way that seemed so much different than the teachings I received in the Catholic, Jehovah's Witness or Christian Churches. We weren't taught to fear God, but only to walk with him in his light. Everybody spoke at the gatherings, even the children. We all interpreted the Bible differently and as long as the interpretations were kept in line with peace love and harmony, all interpretations were welcomed and all respected. Those who wanted to live by their own interpretation simply could without fear of judgment.

Other religions were never shunned, as Rastafari advocated coexistence. We believe that Rastafari is in the heart and not taught. Once you've received it via the ether, you were more accepting to the teachings. I also loved the affinity to Africa, and our deep connection with where my ancestors came from. The use of the many herbs and Magick within this spirituality is similar to how I practice today.

I decided to 'lock' my hair or what some may refer to as dreadlocks, and yes at that early age, I was given a choice to lock or not. I wore Kente tribal print dashiki's and most of the time my hair was wrapped. We wore handmade sandals or would go barefoot during the summertime. We would only eat "Ital" for nourishment. "Ital" derives from the word vital, but in Rastafari this is to signify that certain foods were sacred and vital to the body both spiritually and physically.

I found an affinity with Rastafari, and I felt connected. The reason for the connection was because there were no hardcore rules. Everything is shared, from food, to teachings, and most importantly, love. The community children were one big family with a lot of parents. I felt at home within this community. I had others who were like me and would stand with me whenever we were out in society. I no longer felt alone as I did before.

I never considered Rastafari an organized religion, and many of us in the community felt the same. It was just the way we lived. The Rastafari also revered nature and always lifted the indigent. Our hands were always in the pot when it came to politics, which we believed was a form of oppression. A society that was steeped in politics that oppressed the indigent was referred to as Babylon, and those who flaunted the rules to keep people down were Babylonians.

"Ras" means head, and "Tafari" is the name taken from the Ethiopian King Haile Selassie, who lived during my lifetime from 1930-1974. Tafari was his birth name before his coronation. Growing up some of us believed that Haile Selassie was the descendant of King Solomon. Some believed him to be the incarnation of Jesus Christ. During scripture teaching, some of us would salute him and praise him with "Jah Rastafari!" Jah is taken from Jehovah, meaning God. Some revered him to be "The God", while others in the community received his blessings as Rastafari, simply another human being.

It was weird out there in the big wide world. The "Rasta" was revered by the majority of the West Indian and African cultures. I suppose that was because the ultimate message was one of "Peace and Love" and Bob Marley was a well-known "Ratsta" and respected figurehead.

There were those who thought differently, thinking that we didn't wash, and looked unkempt because we wore our hair in locks. We wore it that way because we believe that there is strength in the hair and the Bible also states *"That no razor shall touch the head until we have lived out our lives on this earth."* (Numbers 6:5.) We also fashioned our hair from the Masai Mara Tribe. The only time we had cause to shave our sacred locks was during the death or passing of an elder or family member. The shaving was a mark of respect and not an attempt to fit in with society.

Another misconception society had about Rastafari was in regard to the "Holy Herb" aka "weed" or "Marijuana." Outsiders thought the adults in our community just smoked all day, and that we were lazy and didn't work. In fact many of us did have jobs, although it was mainly the women, they worked typically as cleaners in the hospitality industry or in the hospitals as cooks and cleaners. Outsiders thought the children were smoking the "Holy Herb" as well. This ignorance was comical to me, but this was the state of society at the time. Herb was respected and never abused. We used herb for cooking, for medicinal purposes, and the elders used it as a form of communication with our ancestors during ritual.

It was mainly the men without jobs, and they were unable to get employment because of their locks. For some Rasta, they simply did not want to work for Babylon. They instead "lived off the land" by growing their own food, and took on odd jobs inside and outside of the community. It was difficult being a Rasta when it came to getting a job to feed your family because of the weed stigma as well.

Unfortunately this stigma was detrimental to me and my siblings. I was teased at school because of my hair and unusual attire. I was even ostracized by a few of my teachers. I had very few friends and stayed most of the time in the presence of my Aunt.

It seemed so funny that society judges you on your appearance and hearsay rather than your skill set. I remember a friend's Mum going for an internal job, but was unable to get it because she had become a Rasta and wore a head wrap to cover her locks. She was able to obtain a job only when she eventually cut her hair.

There were shaman in my community, and their knowledge was vast. Most of the medicinal information was never written, only spoken and passed down for many a generation. Magick was practiced although it was not looked at in that way. It was just seen as a gift, just like Jesus had the gift of healing. If you had these talents it was always welcomed, but never seen as or called Magick, just a gift.

After many years I eventually cut off my locks too. At the time it was difficult for me to do this, because of the

Rasta Belief. After the act of cutting my hair, I felt like I lost a part of me and kept my locks for years before burning during a ritual. I grieved after cutting them, but I knew that I needed to do it to continue my spiritual journey by leaving the community to experience the world. Though I had physically left, my strong beliefs and rituals have never waned.

Even though Rastafari and Voodoo are different in many aspects, there are similarities. They both revere their African roots and heritage, both are advocates for healing, and both practice ritual even if the terminology used is different.

As time passes I encounter many crossroads on my spiritual journey. I even returned to Christianity, but by this time I was grown. I end up attending a Baptist church, which really taught me that the latter was not for me. I started to read about many different religions including Islam and Buddhism, but my journey always lead me back to where I started, Witchcraft. This time, however, it is with Wicca. What sealed the deal for me was the incorporation of Nature, the God/dess. It is with Wicca that I find balance and I feel a sense of belonging like I had never experienced before. Witchcraft is inherent within me.

While studying Wicca, I even put in to prospective some of the Christian teachings I was brought up with, and I now relate to Jesus Christ in a whole new way. He is like many of us: a mystic, a healer, a person who preached love, peace, and truth. He like me, and countless others, was on a path of spiritual learning. His healings were not much different than when I would use ritual to heal.

Regardless of this, I always felt that I never fit in with society. I begin to notice that even though I have no locks or dashiki or anything that identifies me from a particular group, people still regard me as different. I can understand it because of my interests, the way I dress, eat, and view life as a whole creeps into my everyday life and shows itself. I am a Witch. Much of society is not of the pagan persuasion, and once they find out that I am they stop speaking to me altogether. Society and its ignorance have categorized Witchcraft as demonic. Again I am stereotyped, but this time I am no longer hiding in the shadows. After all there cannot be darkness without the light.

 I stand in my power. Now if someone asks me if I am a Witch, I tend to make it more palatable for them by stating I am a Pagan. Society is frightened by the word Witch for some reason. Even though I see a shift of acceptance in society, I still get numerous people who avoid me simply because of my spirituality. This time, however, I am okay with their ignorance and their choice to not associate with me.

 My previous spiritual experiences have allowed me to easily incorporate and amalgamate my rituals to Wicca, simply because of how all-encompassing Wicca/Paganism is. Today I practice and incorporate all that I have learned from my spiritual journey into my ritual. I am eclectic and being this way allows me to view Magick in many ways, and from a variety of angles different from other religions. I have a circle of friends who practice Voodoo, and friends who are Wiccan. I am able to partake in rituals comfortably, because I am not being held accountable to one or the other, but have both love and respect for each. I am overjoyed at where I am today spiritually. I attend many different Pagan rituals and learn new ones all the time, some of which I incorporate into my daily practice. I follow the Wiccan Rede. For the most part I am a solitary Witch, but attend circle with other Witches mostly during sacred events. I am still learning, but the impact of being stereotyped has become unimportant to me now. It took many years but I have let that go. I am going to be me regardless, I came here as me and I will leave as me. The child that was teased and bullied, and the adult who was continuously shunned by others because of her beliefs, are now one. The past has not hindered my future or quest for spirituality, only propelled it.

Bibliography

Messages From Beyond '. "*Ghost Writer. The entity known as Wright. 1990.*
The Bible King James Version. "Numbers 6.5

The Voice of the Ancestors

Alisa Kuumba Zuwena

Love, willpower, support, feminine flowing energy and connecting with ancestral roots can be very powerful healing. I've been blessed to see and have a strong connection to the ancestors. Simply put, I can see and hear those who have passed on. This connection has led to profound healing. It has shaped the course of my life and has helped me help thousands of others.

In Detroit, during the 60's, my family lived on the Westside in a four Family flat. We had a neighbor, by the name of Ruby. She had fish fries and card games on Friday evenings. We all looked forward to this. Ruby had a sister by the name of Ruth. She was full of joy and a lively woman. She was a hairdresser at a shop on Davison near Dexter Avenue. She would often come to these gatherings. We were all very excited when Ruth became pregnant. She gave birth to a beautiful daughter that winter. Not long after the birth, she returned to work. Too quickly many felt. One day, Ruth went outside wearing only a sweater to smoke a cigarette in the dead of winter and caught pneumonia. About three days later, Ruth was dead. When I got the news, I was very sad and afraid of death. I cried and shouted, "I don't want to die!"

During the funeral, friends and family of Ruth walked past the open casket to say goodbye and I was encouraged to do the same. I was terrified. I walked past her and saw her lying there. She appeared to be in a peaceful sleep.

That evening Ruth visited me in the same dress she had been buried in, the lovely light blue, satin, sixties style, form-fitting dress. She sat at the end of my bed. I covered my head hoping that when I took the covers down she would disappear or go back where she came from, but each time I took a look, she was still sitting there.

Ruth spoke to me. She told me not to worry about her. She was doing fine. She told me death was a natural occurrence. I had nothing to fear. She told me she would stay with me until I fell asleep. I eventually fell asleep.

The next morning, I looked for her everywhere, but I never saw her again. What did happen though is that I began to have prophetic dreams about people before they made their transition to the other side. After the experience with Ruth, I had opened a doorway to the other side. My first sign of this was with my sister's godmother, Mrs. Robinson. My brother Duane and I loved her as if she was our godmother. I dreamed of her making her transition one Sunday morning.

As I was dreaming, she was having a heart attack in church. I told everyone about the dream and it scared them. Mrs. Robinson's heart attack was severe. She did not live too long after that Sunday. She transcended within a few months.

That experience made me fearful of telling anyone about dreams of that sort. I had not grown enough to realize that we are always transcending and changing. That it was the natural order of life. After all, we are spirit beings and the spirit lives.

It was a few years before I became more confident and secure in letting someone know of what I dreamt or saw in the spirit or about the other side. I came to understand that ancestors have a way of guiding, protecting and helping us.

Many times before someone passes, their spirit will visit me in my dream state to let me know they are crossing over. They also leave messages for loved ones for me to deliver, and I do. I think this happens because there are words and information that loved ones need to hear. They need peace of mind and resolve. This information helps with the release process, as do the shedding of tears. In many traditions, tears are the cleansing that is necessary for guiding the spirit and healing those left in this realm. The tears allow for healing and remembrance in a healthy holistic way.

It's very important to remember those who came before us. We are them and they are us. We stand on the shoulders of our ancestors. We are the link to the past and the future. Many times we know and do things that we have not been trained for, nor learned in school. This is old energy, ancestral energy that is a part of you. We are helping to work out karma for ourselves and for our ancestors.

I began to pursue my spiritual life in the late seventies. At that time, I did not understand my connection with the ancestors. The early part of my spiritual journey included numerology, astrology, and sitting under a pyramid to get charged from the focal point.

During the 70's, I was very much into the theater life. I was a member of a repertory theater. I worked hard and played hard. There were lots of parties and of course the things that go along with that lifestyle. One night, I dreamed of my Grandmother. She was elegantly dressed in an African Traditional dress. This puzzled me because in life she was a countrywoman. Her style was simple and plain; no ornaments or jewelry. She had a crooked stick wand in her hand. She pointed the stick to the sky and said very firmly "You better straighten up girl!" After that dream, I realized I was not living my life in a fruitful way. I was getting high and not being very responsible.

In 1981 I returned to college to finish my education. I was the president of a school organization and worked often with a young socialist by the name of Joyce. She surprised me one evening when she brought out her tarot cards. At that time in my life, I was terrified of anything that related to a Tarot reading. I had watched too much TV. Joyce helped me overcome my fears. One evening when we were studying she asked me to read her cards. I did. The accuracy rate was 90%. It shocked her and me. I began reading tarot cards for friends and family. I continued to grow and stretch in many directions. I discovered I was very clairvoyant and at times clairaudient (able to hear spirits speaking to me).

In 1986 I moved to New York City to pursue my artistic career. My experiences included performing plays, singing and reading for the American Psychic Association. During those years I met many people who vibrated at a very high spiritual level. Their light was a key for me that opened doors and revealed spiritual gifts that I never knew existed. I had always been looking outside for something that was inside me.

One fall night in Brooklyn, a group of friends and I, who had spiritual *and* artistic gifts, got together and did a show. After the show we shared our spiritual gifts with the audience. A man requested a tarot card reading from me at the event. During the reading he asked me about his health. He asked me to look at him and see if there were any problems. He wanted me to scan his body, to see if I could see any physical problems. I told him I could not do that. He said very firmly, "Yes, you can." Then his body lit up in my mind like an x-ray. I could see he had some problems in the stomach area that were pretty serious. He told me afterward, that what I had described was very accurate. So after that day, I learned I could see health issues.

During the nineties my gift to see the ancestors really flourished. My Ancestors had always been there. Kemetic chants introduced to me by a dear friend connected me to the other side, and to my ancestors. The chant specifically dealt with the universal forces of wisdom from the Old

Ones, the grandmother and grandfather energy. The ancestors, as well as spirit guides, began to come to me. They gave me all sorts of knowledge and messages for myself, and others. So, the most powerful way for me to make contact comes through song/chants sung during their lifetime. There are instances when I will hear and sing tones that are just effective as the songs.

During the last few years, I discovered that honoring the ancestors by pouring libation, as they do in many cultures in Latin America and African countries, was very empowering. Saying their names aloud and thanking them for the gift of life, the gifts of skills, and knowledge from those who preceded us, is very powerful and helpful too. It allows me to understand certain karma families carry through generations and enlightens me on why certain behaviors exist inside your person that you don't understand.

In 1997, I met Mama Jean Taiwo, a world renowned Healer/Spirit Worker, from New Orleans. She taught me that healing is most successful when the whole group involved participates. Before knowing this, I would carry the energy for many people and would feel exhausted for days after doing ceremonies.

Everyone is blessed with a special gift. Some of us feel we have no power or nothing special to offer in a healing situation. We are giving our power away when we think, feel and verbalize these thoughts. Sometimes there is one person in the group who may have very nurturing and mothering qualities. These qualities are very important and necessary. There is nothing like the love of a mother.

In 1996, a good example of total group participation occurred on the beautiful and mystical St. Helena's Island in South Carolina. The hanging moss on century old trees, the marshes, and sweet smells from the foliage in the area, and the very strong ancestral presence, provided the perfect atmosphere for the powerful healing that took place that day. Four healings took place.

One particularly funny incident involved an eighty-year-old woman. She was experiencing pain in her legs and knees. After the healing circle she began to dance. We couldn't stop laughing as we watched her feet move at what seemed to be a hundred miles per hour. Another woman in her early thirties had explained to everyone about the back pain she had been experiencing continuously for almost two months. After prayers, she was able to dance pain-free. The biggest blessing of the day for everyone was clarity and knowing.

The ability to communicate with the ancestors can help others directly and indirectly. A few years ago, I had a client who had been diagnosed with cancer. She was told she had about three months to live. During our session I contacted her ancestors. They gave me a lot of information. She would have to be disciplined and diligent. They told me it was not her time to make a transition. After she left, my human side was terrified for her. I thought of her all night and prayed for her good health. She was the mother of two children. She was a very kind and sweet woman.

After our consultation, she changed her diet, had chemotherapy, and saw a woman known for her "laying on hands" healing abilities. Two years later, she was healthy and cancer-free.

Around 2000, I joined The Trail of Dreams Walkers on the Appalachian Trails. The Trail of Dreams was a global walk for peace led by its visionary, Audri Scott. The peace walk took a small group across the globe in an effort to promote peace among nations.

The first stretch of the walk was the Trail of Tears. This was the path the Cherokee people walked as they left their ancestral land for the reservations. I participated in a small leg at the beginning of what would become literally a walk across the world.

We arrived in Hot Springs and the campsite was beautiful. Our tents were pitched next to the river. After we set up tents, we had sandwiches and snacks that evening. We tried hard to get the campfire going, but all we could get was a flicker. We assumed it was because of the dampness coming from the river.

After eating, we sang to the ancestors. We sang old church songs and Native-American chants. When the prayers and songs are sincere, the results for this kind of sacred circle can be very powerful. Non-believers have had a change of heart after this type of spiritual work because of the blessings and interesting happenings that come forth. The blessings and info that comes forth is private, intimate, or only info that someone who has transcended knows about the person.

At the campsite, a very powerful Native American Healer came through, Mountain Eagle Woman. The Trail of Dreams had been her vision. After her messages and blessings of love and warmth, we went to bed. The next morning, many of us had a lot to talk about. After we all had gone to sleep, or let's say *tried* to go to sleep, the campgrounds had come alive that night. The fire was ablaze. We kept hearing laughter and conversation, but whenever we would look out of our tents, we would see nothing.

Dee-Dee informed us that while walking down the road, she heard footsteps behind her. She thought one of us was playing with her. She turned her flashlight upon what she thought was somebody and to her surprise they disappeared. We all laughed at this phenomenon—the ancestors had a party as we attempted to sleep that night by the river.

After all those events, we had a circle of healing and discussed what had taken place. The ancestors blessed us with a lot of healing and emotional release that morning. They have guided me these past few years and healed me also.

In November 1999, a group of powerful spiritual folk gathered at my home one evening. Mama Jean was visiting and doing spiritual work in Atlanta. The ancestors came through several of the participants during the healing ritual. The very next day I was called by Emory Hospital for a kidney transplant. I had been on dialysis for five years before that special week.

The love of family and friends, and most importantly, the ancestors, healed me. The god/goddess-mother-father energy and the ancestors carried me through those difficult years with the spirit. The energy allowed me luxuries with my poor health that other dialysis patients never experience. I traveled to Senegal, Africa. I went camping and did manual peritoneal dialysis in the Rocky Mountains in Colorado. Yes, I allowed myself to enjoy life's experiences. The ancestors held me up, as they can hold all of us on their shoulders.

Remembering and honoring our ancestors can enhance and empower our lives in ways you can't imagine. There are many ways to honor the ancestors. Many cultures have one thing in common, pouring libation.

Here is a simple and easy way to honor your ancestors. You will need a container of water. If possible a small hand held bell is good. Ring the bell as you sprinkle and/or pour water on a living plant or the ground. To invoke the Ancestral energy say: "I'd like to honor the Ancestors of the Land, of the Blood and of the Spirit". You may continue honoring your Ancestors by calling or thinking their names, while pouring water after each name on the ground, into the earth or on a plant.

When we forget our Ancestors, they cannot help us. Like a tree without roots, it dies. When we remember and keep their spirit alive, the results are limitless and powerful.

Starting Small

Flame Bridhesdottir

When first I started down my twisty Pagan path, I took baby steps. To say my practice was simple would be an understatement. Because everything was so new to me, I spent most of my time reading and learning; my acts of devotion and ritual were mainly connected with my growing awareness of and belief in the Divine as Immanent.

Therefore, talking to the moon, rambling around the yard with my cat, planting flowers, tending my herbs, and walking in the woods by the creek became my daily devotions. The most elaborate I got was lighting a candle and some incense while I meditated.

As my knowledge and contact with other Pagans grew, so did my practice, and with it, my doubts. The more information I absorbed, the more I thought I wasn't doing enough; not meditating enough, not praying enough, not offering enough. Not Black enough.

The latter was reinforced by the many people who automatically assumed I would naturally practice one of the African Traditional Religions; then there were the people who would relay messages to me from the Ancestors, in which I was told that my path lay within the ATRs. Around this same time I was developing an interest in Hoodoo, an African-American system of folk magic. While I found the uses and ascribed properties of various herbs and curios fascinating, I was immediately put off by the heavy use of the Bible. I no longer cultivated a relationship with Christian deities, and was uncomfortable evoking them during workings. In an attempt to resolve my internal conflict, I talked to a number of Hoodoo practitioners, some of whom treated the Bible as simply another grimoire. Mostly I encountered people who seemed offended that I was even taking issue with the Bible. The prevailing sentiment was, "If you have a problem with the Bible, then Hoodoo is not for you", with a strong suggestion that I lacked gravitas and commitment, was simply rebelling against Christianity, and was a religious bigot to boot.

In my attempt to follow advice and keep my Hoodoo practice true to its roots, I found myself more and more spiritually disconnected. The complicated rituals, and sometimes days long workings, were a far cry from the humble but heartfelt magic I had practiced in the past. The psalms were ashes in my mouth. The biggest obstacle for me though turned out to be political; I could not bring myself to utilize the very book that had been used to justify slavery and oppress Blacks, in my personal spiritual practice in which I was trying to honor my ancestors.

On one hand I was avidly curious about magical systems in general, on the other hand I began to mentally balk anytime a working required the Bible, a psalm, or evocations of angels or Christian deities. As a result, I stopped practicing altogether. I was getting no comfort or joy from my spiritual practices. Devotional activities ceased. No candles were lit, no incense burned, no offerings made. I was trapped in a spiritual no-man's-land, a liminal state, trying to honor both my Black and White ancestry and eventually, in my despair, failing to honor either one.

When what seemed an unending series of calamitous events over the ensuing three years only served to drive me further into myself, I stopped even attending events in the Pagan community. I withdrew from online discussion groups, and stopped updating my blog. I became a Pagan in Name Only. When losing our home to foreclosure devastated me, I packed up my altar, my herbs and oils and powders, my books and candles. Since relocating, I've left it all packed.

I've decided to go back to the simple practices that brought me so much happiness. I'm starting small. I like to feed the birds in the morning, and talk to the moon at night. My relationship with one of my cats has unexpectedly flourished. Zelda (who ignored me like paint on a wall the first three years of her life) is now my constant companion; her devotion is astonishing. I reciprocate with treats and early morning games of fetch. We take long rambly walks in the moonlight together, exploring the night world. Our new rapport has done more to reaffirm my faith than anything else in the past three years.

I had forgotten that ultimately my spirituality is between me and the Gods. I did them no favors by going through the motions, and I cheated myself of the comfort and aid that might have made these past few rough years easier to bear. So in my effort to discover where my path might end, I have come back to where it began.

When the weather warms, I'll once again plant my flowers and herbs, and walk in the woods by the creek; maybe I'll even set up a little altar with a candle and some incense.

Right now though, it's time to play fetch with Zelda.

Do You Even Know Me?

Olivia Haynes

I started writing Black Witch because, despite looking high and low, I could not find any dedicated media for Black Pagans. I'm a strong believer in representation and its effect on their respective groups. It was and still is important to me to create media that was made for the intersection of Paganism and Blackness because the issues that plague Black Pagans are not going to match the issues of a White Pagan exactly. Regularly, I hear from Black Pagan readers who are happy that Black Witch exists because finally there is media directed at them and made by a Black person. They can finally have media that is not an obvious afterthought on inclusiveness or by someone who does not understand the complexities of Black culture. The readers are happy that I, too, am a Black Pagan because there are certain parts of our existence and experience that has to be lived - not simply studied or discussed to shreds - to intricately know and understand.

There is a familiar saying: "you can't be it if you can't see it". I agree with this sentiment strongly, especially since history has been regularly Whitewashed and modified far past recognition just to make sure that minorities don't get the spotlight they deserve repeatedly. In Paganism, this can - and does - actively dissuade minorities from being Pagan, or to join in with others. In addition, white-washing subtly convinces White Pagans that they are the only ones "worthy" and "knowledgeable" enough about the gods to interact with them while reinforcing distorted beliefs about minorities and their cultures. It's important that people see themselves, their heritage and their history as much as possible and without deprecating filters. It is not divisive to focus on what makes us different because, simply put, we're not all the same and it is best not to pretend that we are. It is the erasure of authentic facets of identity that is divisive, not the acknowledgement of our differences.

It is fairly self-evident that the face of Paganism depicts itself as White and at least middle class, almost regardless of tradition. I remember being in bookstores in the Pagan/New Age section and even if the book was about Native American shamans or Voodoo root work, the author was always White. It would both strike me as both unusual and bothersome because it was evident erasure of authentic display of identity. It is not that hard to find a Native American skilled in shamanism to talk about their tribe's practices or a Black person from America or Haiti that could discuss in minute detail the background, conduct and history of root work. It always would seem so roundabout to find a White person to talk about a culture they most likely never grew up in and definitely do not understand the nuances of. It was as if the publishers didn't want to showcase different faces, just pickings here and there from different cultures, and treat those cultures as if they can be absolutely divorced from the people who created them. This practice inadvertently silences the indigenous voices of these cultures and continues to support the face of Whiteness as if "White" means "expert", even if they are not. What's more, these books avoid words like "colonialization", "imperialism" and "cultural genocide" because it would be far too self-aware in what the writer is performing and the publisher is allowing: cultural appropriation.

Being a minority and Pagan, it can be tough because you're never truly accepted by the crowd. No matter how progressive any group paints themselves, there will be groupthink and if it is a mostly White crowd, the groupthink is going to reflect the Anglo-centric society at large. This means, instead of being perceived as a regular person, you may be seen with suspicion, treated as if you're an ambassador of your people or as the personification of someone's media-fed fears and treated as such. You will be exposed to micro-aggressions ("Oh no, not you, you're not like other Black people", "Paganism doesn't cover African faiths") or micro-invalidations ("I don't see color, we're all human", "We're in a post-racial America now, we have a Black president"). The double consciousness is alive and well here because history is forever depicted with a White person being a major part of the narrative somehow and everyone else is a side character and, of course, that belief does get projected.

Sharing culture and history with other Pagans means you're giving yourself and your background a voice, which is important. History is rife with stories: comedic stories, riveting stories, scary stories, stories that make humanity sound ever improving, stories that make humanity sound ever self-destructing. And these stories are filled with a whole lot more than White people. It's important to share these stories to let everyone know that these stories did exist and that they are just as valid an experience as any and every experience. History is filled with amazing stories and most of them are shadowed away because it doesn't completely fit with a mainstream ideology, which usually centers on Whiteness. Sharing culture and history makes it so that everyone gets on the same page and doesn't simply see each other as humans, but as people with different backgrounds that interact in various ways, good, bad and depends-on-who-you-ask. Also, when sharing culture and history to other minorities, it can make for insightful conversations - as long as they don't descend into what is often called "The Suffering Olympics", where various racial or ethnic groups contest who had it worse and thus who should be able to mope the most.

Sharing the collective past of your race, you can be met with blowback, of course. Talk too much about your history and culture and how it has affected people to this very day, prepare to be coined as "angry" (even if you talk calmly) or with a "chip on your shoulder" and how you make others uncomfortable because for once, there is a story where Whiteness is not the good guys saving the day but quite possibly the bad guy instead. You may make someone cry, get unnecessarily angry or told that you should choose between your "militancy" and getting along with everyone. It's exceedingly rare to find the one White Pagan that actually understand the different and intricate complexities and intersections of race and religion and thus are capable of giving space and being truly empathetic.

I think what is also possibly understated prior is that minorities can also interact with each other and share their cultures and histories, along with their perspectives. No one should be around to neither educate the masses nor serve as the cultural ambassador if they don't want to be, it can be just as nice to talk about your experiences without providing explanations. Not everyone had the same history and it's imperative to learn about others, particularly those of the historically marginalized. And it is important to remind everyone that history did not always go along the pattern of things being okay and then the White people arrived. Various groups had issues or squabbles or wars with each other, it is important to not paint with a broad brush. Does this mean that White Privilege and its damage is fictional? Nope, White privilege is still as real as the grass that grows in a meadow; it just means that there is more to the story of the world than what is centered on the construct of Whiteness and the people that regularly benefit from it.

It is inspiring and very reassuring to see yourself represented in media and especially in religious practice.

Not to see images of your identity through a modified and over-racialized perspective but just as you are. It is important for minority Pagans to experience seeing themselves displayed in mainstream Pagan culture and not as half-earnest side attempts at general diversity. To have genuine, diverse representation – not empty lip service - would create safer spaces for minority Pagans. When we see that the face of Paganism is White and so are the faces of the deities, regardless of home culture, it creates a sense of "Whites Only", which can make minority Pagans feel uncomfortable, ostracized and alone. It is important to avoid having a lip service type of diversity because it isn't really diversity when people of different faces are allowed but their complete cultures and their experiences aren't. To display genuine inclusiveness would not only greatly reduce frustrations and feelings of not belonging, it would also improve multicultural relations and understandings between Pagans, especially for those who need to be heard the most.

To note, not every interaction with another culture is cultural appropriation. A very basic guideline between cultural appreciation and cultural appropriation:

Cultural appropriation: When an object or concept of culture is taken out of context (such as a war bonnet or Black slang) to be exploited and/or reduced in overall appreciative value. Also, the originators of the cultural object or concept are consistently silenced, demonized, ignored or removed altogether.

Cultural appreciation: Inclusive of the originators of the cultural object or concept. The object or concept is not only introduced but so are the contexts, the creators and the identities that accompany them. And not only are they introduced, they are given the respect of being noted as authentic in opposed to exaggerated or as secondary to the mainstream.

It is also important to note that not every person is an

ambassador of their background nor knows everything there is to know about their history. This does not render their lived experience invalid but it does not mean they're going to know the ins and outs of institutionalize racism, the intricate history of racism, the present day effects of that intricate history of racism and the various intersections they can come in. That can only be learned though dedicated study of social issues and discussion. Besides, there is no race ambassador. However, just because there isn't a race ambassador, that does not mean there aren't any noted intellectuals and academics that have dedicated their minds and lives to the study of prejudice and its various intersections.

It is important to share and express various cultures and histories to best diversify Paganism and to show a different perspective. The more people talk, the more they offer a well-needed voice to the overall mainstream Pagan experience. It is important that Paganism is not centered on Whiteness because it won't help the religion at all: actually the opposite. When different cultures are whitewashed and used as decoration, so much harm is caused. This is not simply exposure because whitewashing invalidates and otherizes those cultures, not show them as they are. It is imperative that there is more than one story to every experience. Without sharing those additional stories or actively silencing or dismissing them, the faith is going to appear continually fractured because people want to join a new faith that works in sync with who they are, not make them think they have to give up one part of their identity for another.

A Candle for Remembrance: A Juneteenth Working

Crystal Blanton

Standing in the present, on the ground of history and with one foot in the future, I hold the significance of today in my heart and my mind.

To step into a future with willful intent, I must acknowledge the size of the step before me, and shine a light so that I can see it.

My past is as important as my future, for my ancestors are as relevant to my story as my children.

And so I light this candle in remembrance of the souls that died in physical, spiritual, social and mental pain....

I light this candle in remembrance of the children who watched the horror of slavery become their future.

I light this candle for the women who were taken again and again.

I light this candle for the men that were broken time after time.

I light this candle for the generations that have carried this pain in their psyche, a part of their unconscious schema.

I light the candle for those who fought and died before tasting freedom.

I light this candle for those who STILL fight.

I light this candle for all that experience the horror of history manifest throughout time, and through generations.

I light this candle for my White brothers and sisters today that carry the guilt of a pain they did not cause.

I light this candle for my Black brothers and sisters that know not who they are and are fighting through a whitewashed world to find the root of their souls.

I light this candle for JUSTICE.

I light this candle for the revolutionary then and now.

I light this candle for them.
I light this candle for you.
I light this candle for our children.
I light this candle for me.
I light this candle for healing.
And so it is… and it shall be.
ALL POWER TO THE PEOPLE FOREVER, So mote it be.

Who Are You and What Do You Do?

Szmeralda Shanel

What's in a name?

In many ways my work as a priestess has changed since moving from the San Francisco Bay area back to my mother city Chicago. For one, I find that I use the title priestess a lot less often when I am describing who I am and what I do. In Chicago the community that I serve come from various spiritual traditions, most of them are not Pagan and some of them don't even know what a Pagan is. To these people priestess has little meaning or when it does, they often assume that as a priestess I work only with people who are a part of my religious tradition.

For the most part, the people that I work with already have their religion. They are coming to me for guidance and support around practical things like love, money, or work. Sure some of them are concerned about what a particular dream may have meant or are looking for help with finding the right spiritual path for themselves. But most of them want to know how they can get unstuck from and move through a current situation that is causing them suffering. They want to know what the likely outcome will be if they make certain choices and how they can make important changes in their lives.

They do not care what my religion or spiritual practice is. No one cares who initiated me into what; they are not interested in who I pray to, where I pray or how. When someone comes to see me what they care about is whether my readings are accurate, and whether the tools that I give them are effective. Basically does the work, work? And for this reason, while I certainly am still a priestess, when I tell people what it is I do, these days, I refer to myself as a spiritual worker. Around here folks tend to know what that means and they will usually say "Oh okay, now what kinds of work do you do?", and we go from there.

This is not to say that I never use the term priestess. If someone is really interested in sitting down and getting to know me, then there is time to talk about who I am as a person, why I am a priestess, what I do and what it all means. You will also hear me speak of myself as a priestess if I'm teaching a spiritual workshop, leading a ritual circle or officiating a wedding ceremony. But when someone sits down at my table and they need to know what they can do for protection, to shift their bad luck, or see if a certain person is trustworthy, I'm a spiritual worker.

The people who know me well also know that I am a Witch, I am not and have never been closeted, however, you won't really hear me using that term either these days simply because it is another word that causes confusion. In my experience, the folks who know that Witch does not mean devil worshipper assume that being a Witch means I am Wiccan and I am not. So again, you'll only really hear me talking to someone about this if they are really interested in getting to know me as a person. I've noticed that as the years go by, I am less interested in educating people about my work and spirituality, and unless someone is sincerely seeking or genuinely interested, I just don't have the time or desire to explain all these things.

Excuse me, but who let Jesus up in here?

I have also found that before, when it came to working with spirits, I used the words Gods and Goddesses more often. But since returning home there are many different types of spirits supporting me in my work. For this reason, these days if I'm speaking in general terms I am more likely to say "the spirits" or "the mysteries" than "The

Goddesses and Gods".

One spirit that has found his way back on an altar in my house is Jesus. I'm guessing he never really went anywhere and has just been hanging around rubbing his hands together with a little smile, all like, "Oh you gonna let me back in the house sooner or later little lady." It's not that I have a problem with Jesus, I was raised a Christian and Jesus is the first spirit I had a relationship with. I loved him, we got along well, and when I decided to leave the church and Christianity I left on good terms with J.C. While I have respect for his teachings, I knew and still know, Christianity is not my path or spiritual home.

Working within the Hoodoo tradition, Jesus was always in my house to a certain extent but he ended up getting a permanent space on the altar when my grandparents died. My grandfather was a Pentecostal preacher, and he and my grandmother had a Sanctified church in Alabama. When I was growing up my brothers and I stayed with our grandparents for the whole summer every year. In their church I witnessed them practice the spiritual gifts of prophecy, laying on of hands, Holy Ghost possession, and speaking in tongues. People were prayed over, anointed with oil, and at certain times the church did a communal foot washing ceremony where everyone's feet were washed while singing a song about being washed in the blood of the lamb. I had mixed feelings about what I saw in the church, I thought it was all kind of strange, some of it scary, some of it fascinating.

I did not know what any of it meant, I did know that all healing was done in the name of Jesus. But the things happening in this church were much different than the things that happened at our church back in Chicago. I remember sitting with my brothers in those old wooden pews on Sundays from early morning til late into the night, playing the tambourine and singing. Other pew activities included napping, getting wide eyed and nervous when someone sitting nearby would get to shoutin and fallin out, and trying not to get pinched by our grandma for playing and giggling. And then there were the times when the three of us would sit quietly, crunching on apples or sucking on butterscotch and peppermint candies from the old ladies purses. With a sense of fear and awe we'd watch our Pa Pa do amazing things. He had a lot of spiritual power.

By the time I was old enough to ask my grandparents more about the hows and whys of what went on in their church, I had already left the Christian tradition and had no interest in learning about what they did in their church. I was so busy arguing about the things that weren't right about Christianity that I missed out on learning first hand some of the magic within it. I now regret my arrogance.

Before she died, I was able to ask my grandmother how they did the laying on of hands healing. She said "You just pray. Jesus told the disciples they could do it, and so we can." I just kind of shrugged at that, I was looking for some kind of technique. But after she died I had a dream in which she appeared and told me that I could do this work. Thank you grandma.

My ancestors know as well as I do that I am not and have never really been Christian material. I know I will never return to that path, it is not my way. But another thing I've learned and now know without a doubt is this; I can NOT be a Christian all I want, but since the death of my grandparents, what I CANNOT do is have an ancestor altar up that does not include a cross or a picture of Jesus and my Granddaddy's Bible. Period. Believe me I tried and now I know better. So basically, Jesus is back in my house y'all.

Practice Practice Practice

When I was living in the Bay area a lot of my spiritual practice consisted of working with groups facilitating public seasonal, lunar and rites of passage rituals done within the Pagan community. Today in Chicago I work mostly one on one with people who are not a part of the Pagan community. My work consists of magical coaching/consulting, intuitive readings, cleansing and healing work, and spiritual counseling. As an artist who is deeply aware of the healing power of the arts and creative process, it is as common for my clients to leave a session with me with a prescription for journal writing, painting, drumming or singing as it is to leave with instructions to set up and work at an ancestor altar, write a petition paper or dress and burn a certain candle. Outside of a women's dark moon circle that I co-facilitate with another priestess, and various spiritual and expressive arts workshops that I teach, I do very little group work in the Pagan community these days.

While I did participate in rituals for the 8 seasonal sabbats when I lived in California, I've honestly never felt much of a connection with Celtic wheel of the year. For me the holy days are about celebrating and connecting with my community and while some of my community is Pagan, my family and many of my friends are not. What makes most sense to me, and what I feel the most connection to are the basic traditional American-style holidays.

In November I do Thanksgiving with friends and family, that's my harvest festival. I do Christmas with presents and food and lights, that's my winter holiday. In February I usually do something special with Brigid because she is a Goddess close to my heart. Come springtime I dye eggs, share chocolate, eat a lil' ham, rabbit, or lamb and celebrate spring with everyone else, usually at Easter. I am an indulgent woman and love the lusciousness of Beltane, so sometimes I do something. Summer Solstice is nice but my big summer celebration is spent with my people eating barbeque and watching fireworks on the 4th of July. I love Halloween and that's what I call it. I also do an ancestor feast usually in October or November.

There are other holy days during the year but they are usually to honor specific spirits, ancestors, teachers, etc. and these honoring ceremonies happen on the person's birth or death day. My birthday is January 15th, same as Dr. Martin Luther King Jr, and he is always honored with a special ritual at my birthday. In fact while most of my friends and family are Christian or non religious, they are all very open and will tell you "We have to get to Shanel's birthday parties on time because she has activities for us to do." *Activities* means rituals, and everyone participates.

Last year a friend was in town and asked me to host a winter solstice party. I did and we were all just hanging out drinking vodka, dancing and eating snacks when someone asked me "So are we going to do something? You know, some kind of activity?" I said, "Well, I hadn't planned anything because I thought we were just having a party but I can if people want to." People were very interested in doing something so we had small simple ritual that people were invited but not pressured to participate in. Everyone did and afterwards many people pulled me to the side throughout the night and said "Hey thanks, I really needed to do something like that."

I have noticed a bit of shifting in some of my beliefs about things that I was once very certain of. While this has been confusing and frustrating at times, for the most part I've found it exciting. As a person who can be pretty stubborn and prideful at times, I sometimes worry that as I learn more and get older I will become rigid and full of self-importance. When a strongly held belief shifts a little and I understand it differently or don't understand it at all, I know that I am still open to the many possibilities that are. I am reminded that while I know and understand a lot of things, there are many, many things that I don't know, am still learning and will never completely know or understand. Holding this in my awareness, I am able to work at balancing pride with humility.

These days for the most part my practice looks a lot just like being in the world, and doing what I can with the skills that I have. It also means pointing people in the direction of one who can better assist them when I don't have the knowledge or skills to help them. My practice is regular work at my altar sitting with myself to better know the truth of who I am and to develop stronger relationships with my spirits so that I can better understand their guidance. It also means continuing to learn from the elders in the traditions that I am a part of, my loved ones and the world around me.

Foxtrot in Flames

Pablo Vazquez III

Borne between the burning horizons
A savage beauty in eternal supernovas
An image insurmountable in my vision
Though my heart swims in crimson blood
I dare not drown in your infernal beauty

The raging cries of a thousand stares
Where demons grasp towards shining Empyrean
Funneling inwards through Arcadian craft
Towards Nirvana in the core of a distant star
Untouchable as Greek Fire in destined flight

Bind me to the prisons of Xibulba!
With impish insult and daemonic scorn
Eris conquers all in blazing fury
Through grand aetherial phoenix's flight
Mine heart's stellar darkness be purged.

Honoring Ancestors When You Don't Know Who They Are

Alexandra Chauran

"Ancestor worship is an important part of every Pagan Path." That's about when I start tuning out from whatever book I am reading. I like to say that I'm half gypsy and half inbred in the south for hundreds of years. Gypsy, of course, being inappropriate slang for the Romani people almost certainly in my bloodline somewhere, wanderers of Europe, and "inbred in the south" is my only understanding of the confused family tree of my embarrassed and secretive grandparents on my mom's side. On my father's side, my great-grandparents were killed by Nazis. My drunk and angry grandmother didn't want to talk about her family. I heard stories that my grandparents travelled by foot from the Ukraine and Poland to Portugal to take a boat to Canada after witnessing family being killed in a barn. Were they Romani? Were they Jews? I don't know. I don't even know their names, and no churning of genealogy software will conjure them. All I know is that my dark-skinned father didn't consider himself white enough for the Rosicrucians and that kids in school used to play "guess her ethnicity" with me with shout-outs ranging from islander to Latina.

This isn't to say that I am not interested in the names of my ancestors and their stories. I believe in reincarnation and I believe in spirits, so it stands to reason that I am very spiritually motivated to be able to recognize the ghosts of my ancestors or to meet them again after they are reborn into their new bodies. I stand in complete envy when I see coveners pull out black and white photographs of distant relations and place them on the altar at Samhain. I nearly turned green when I heard somebody brag about how his great-great-some-amount-of-greats stepmom was Cleopatra. I even went down to my local Church of Jesus Christ of Latter Day Saints to use their free resources for family research, an option which I highly recommend.

It may seem weird, then, that I once decided to torture myself by RSVPing for a Samhain ancestor worship celebration with my local Vodou and Ifa celebrants. The invitation said that I should bring photographs of all of my known ancestors and some food that they would have enjoyed in life. At the time I owned precisely zero photographs of deceased relatives and had not yet invited any to dinner to see what they enjoyed. So, I hazarded a guess by heading to the local Polish grocery store and picking up a box of eastern European candies. Everyone likes candy, right?

At the ritual, the gates were opened with an appeal to Papa Legba, the shrines to the lwa seemed alive in leaping candlelight and an ancestor shrine was overflowing with home cooked foods made with secret family recipes. I covered my head with a white hat and kept my heels together to prevent unintentional spirit possession as drums raised the energy and made us all seem to enter the world of the dead. As the Mambo leading the ceremonies directed, people around the circle began to raise their voices, naming their ancestors. I began to panic, at the time only knowing the names of two grandparents who were deceased. Everyone's ancestors seemed to be an endless army standing behind them, and the long list of names rolled off tongues like some ancient spell.

I was the last to speak, and when it came time for me to call out to my ancestors, I boldly spoke the first names I knew for my grandparents, feeling inadequate. I knew that my grandmother's name wasn't even her birth name, but one she took on when she immigrated, perhaps to fit in or to hide from her past. I stood awkwardly in the silence for a few beats before the Mambo clapped her hand on my shoulder and finished with, "...and all those ancestors, known and unknown, named and unnamed, on whose shoulders we stand. Ashe." In that moment, I knew that I was accepted. We danced, we ate, and everyone politely complemented me on my store bought candy. Don't feel left out. Here is a ritual that you can perform in order to honor ancestors, even if you don't know who they are.

Ancestor Rite

This rite is best performed after dark on Samhain, but can be used at any time. The minimal equipment needed for this rite is a surface to make into an altar, a glass of water, and a way to define the circle space such as a ring of flour poured upon the ground. Optional embellishments can include candles, decorations from your ancestors' countries of origin, if known, and any pictures or artifacts from any known ancestors. After my dad died, I used a photograph of him, his watch, and a bottle of his cologne. It is also highly recommended to make a food offering. You can make a dish from your ancestor's country of origin, if known, but there is also something to be said about collecting parts of the ancestor feast from ordinary meals throughout the day. For example, taking to the ritual some cereal from breakfast, a half a sandwich from your lunch, and a small plate of food from the dinner table.

Define the circle. I like to perform this ritual outside, and to pour flour in a circle to define the space. Decorate your altar with anything you have, and place the food and water offering there. Stand a moment in meditation. You may choose to dance in order to raise energy. Then, invoke your ancestors, beginning with any names that you do know.

"I invoke the ancestral spirits of [NAMES, and] all those known and unknown, named and unnamed, on whose shoulders I stand. Be now with me in blood and bone, in mind and heart, in your spirit and in your strength. Thank you."

Break apart your feast foods. Leave a bit of each food on the offering plate and partake of the rest of the food yourself in complete silence. This practice is called a dumb feast, and it is during this time that you may sense the presence of your ancestors and receive messages from them. When you have completed the feast, extinguish any flames and take any valuables with you, but leave the offering plate and the glass of water for the spirits.

Multicultural Paganism: How to Find Your Way

Rose Skye

When I was fifteen, I fell in with a group of teens who discovered witchcraft at roughly the same time – from Crowley to Ride the Silver Broomstick, they had read the lot and took their inspiration from books as well as a few movies on the way. Yeah, I know, but it worked – we didn't know what "chaos" was, although it was pretty akin to what we did. Many pagan and witchy folk I know admit under duress they did the same thing along their own path (most of which involves stumbling around in the dark) – but I had some additional challenges. I'm interracial; I can trace my background to at least seven different cultures. During the 80's everyone I spoke to wanted to know why a "black" kid was interested in Wicca.

Cultural religion as a base-point for practice is a subject many people want to avoid in pagan circles; partly due to its sometimes racist overtones, but also due to cultural appropriation by opportunists. It's certainly understandable why many people balk when someone who doesn't obviously "look like us" attends a spiritual gathering, especially when someone attends one pow-wow or a sweat and then professes they're a shaman. But I don't feel we can pretend racism doesn't exist. Since humans have been on the planet a few thousand years now and we're still hung up on skin color, gender roles and stereotypes, I don't think silence is going to help much.

All of my life I've been told my art, writing, or spiritual beliefs should follow along with "my people", although who "my people" actually are seems to fluctuate in the eye of the beholder. Everyone sees something different in my features – usually the "alien" part they don't recognize as their own race. I grew up having to pick the "black" box in ethnic background questionnaires because at the time the "inter-racial" box didn't exist. "You look black to me!" was the cheery response (usually by white people) as they filled in forms for me, and I just had to smile thinly and take it. However, African-American people always remarked on my "good hair" – not always with approval – while they picked "white". Most Native Americans didn't pick any of the boxes and would say "You're one of us, but we're not sure from where", although to a few I was *waisechu* and that was that. Social identity was difficult enough at the time. When I realized I no longer found anything I could relate to with Christianity, I floundered along many different paths and belief systems, constantly trying to find a niche, which I wasn't sure existed with someone as mixed a racial background as mine. I felt like the Jane of all races, yet the descendant of none.

I did not choose Oya as a patroness – I didn't even give the traditions of Yoruba a look in. At the time, I was desperately trying to deny the African-American side of my heritage. This was partly due to all the Goddess art I had ever seen back then; the Goddess was obviously a beautiful white woman with flowy hair. But if there's one thing my Path has taught me, it's this: sometimes, you don't get a choice about Who calls you. Sometimes, the Powers That Be just choose you, and that's that. Oya made herself more and more known to me, often rather destructively. I had to just face up to it: She chose me. It was a difficult road to Oya, not just because of my own denial, but all the anger and hurt I had to heal up for a half of my culture which went out of its way to let me know how little I belonged due to my traitorous hazel eyes.

This year, I found myself being thrown headfirst into

a belief system with other Powers That Be I have spent a lot of time avoiding, for much the same reasons. I'm half-black, what in the world could I possibly be doing with Norse deities?! Everything I had encountered about the heathen community did not endear me to the idea of working with the system – I will admit I had mostly come across racists and skinheads hiding behind a folkish heathen veneer. The fact my mother's side of the family is Norwegian and Irish (the Norwegian line is very strong) didn't really matter to either me or the heathens I had encountered; I still "look black" to them. Yet once again I realized I didn't really have a choice in the matter – when Thor decides you're one of His, He's difficult to ignore. I found myself throwing my hands up in an "Oh *fine!*" sort of way and just got on with studies and Work, determined to grit my teeth and get on with it.

It's incredible – I've been doing Work for over 30 years now and every year I find I have more to learn. Every time, I come up along a new beginning, a new journey, a new challenge to take on where I fumble around in the dark and try and get my bearings. Every time I feel like a novice without a clue, and I find I have to unlearn, relearn, or just plain *learn* all over again. The first steps of my practice has involved explaining my exotically-blended facial features at a blot – but years of dealing with the same reaction at nearly every single pagan gathering I've been to meant I was well prepared. I can recite family up to seven generations back on my mother's side; my father's is more difficult as slave records were rarely kept to keep slaves from being traced, but I've managed to piece quite a bit together. I have the blood of English cavaliers, French and Norwegian aristocrats, Ashanti-warrior-women and Lenape elders in my veins. I'm descended from a long line of strong women who often raised their children by themselves, and stood up for their people when no one else would. I've learned just how rich my history is, how varied my background. Attending a sweat with my lodge mother several years ago, she told me she had been gifted the vision of seeing my lineage. "You go far back, girl," she said with a note of awe in her voice. I didn't understand her then, but I understand now.

I first felt the insistence of ancestry-recitation at blots would just be a way to try and claim superiority. Now, I won't lie and say there aren't groups out there who are more interested in Aryan purity than anything else. But I've had the honor of working with people who look at ancestry in another way entirely. To know one's bloodlines carries a lot of weight among the heathen community, not for the sake of "purity" but from the concept that one's ancestors are always with us, and are never forgotten. Who we come from defines to an extend who we are – our *wyrd* ties into the deeds and workings of those grand-parents and great-grandparents much removed who came before us, and what we will leave to our children when we are gone. It's an important thread, and can help us live our lives and work off some of that wyrd-debt so our children have a better life.

The second thing which came up in my practice caught me by surprise. It's rarely spoken of that Thor himself is multi-racial, born of an Aesir father and Jotun mother. I have no idea why I didn't figure this out until I delved further into Northern-trad paganism, but I found I understood Thor more than I had previously thought. I had always considered him just a bit of a thick-headed bruiser with quite a few comedic stories about his antics. But the more I've practiced and studied, the more I have come to insights not just upon Thor's more obvious attributes, but what it meant to be born from two peoples in my Norse mythos. There's difficulty of course – as Thor is regularly consigned by his father to fight and kill the race of his mother – but there's also a kinship there which allows Thor to bridge the gap between Jotun and Aesir. He is who He is, and makes no apologies for it.

It's all been rather eye-opening, and I'm aware I'm currently only scratching the surface of my practice, but it has made me wonder of late what my generation and many generations beyond will be doing if they follow the Pagan path. More and more multi-cultural children are being born every day – my son is British-born and bred but is such an exotic-looking child people always comment on it. I have made it a point to try and teach my son as much about my family as I could, sharing my knowledge with him, but I do so with a qualm. Would anyone believe he had the right to attend a feast to Oya, or a pow-wow? Would his English accent mark him as being a "culture vulture"? I have no answers; I just hope I'll have taught child enough that he can recite the names of our kin for those who would question. If that's enough for them, well and good – if not, well he only has to answer to his own Powers That Be.

The first step on your journey as a person studying a belief system out of the norm is always the hardest. I can only say this for any other multi-racial folk out there just starting out: your Powers That Be will choose you regardless of your culture, heritage or background. They'll be the ones you answer to. Sometimes we do not get to choose where our calling comes from. You'll have to deal with explaining this to people – and probably explaining this a lot. You'll have to develop the necessary thick-skin and keep persevering if your path really is in the direction it seems to be going. Be honest with yourself, and be sincere.

I wish you well on your journey; wave at me when you walk by.

Conjuring Woman

Sandra Santiago

Conjuring woman
is *agua bendita* soul,
daughter of diaspora dust,
doesn't not blow in the wind.
She is gathered in molecules
of pressed memories,
conjoined through heart and bone.
You are white doves and black *calderos*
as the *santos* hang from her neck

Conjuring woman
moves in unlit spaces,
argues in the voices of the dead,
wanders in the company of the ancestors,
through the territory of
her name.

Conjuring woman
speaks without moving lips.
Movimiento is language.
El aire becomes a dense,
polyphonic fugue of
ancestral tableaus that trail back
through nude primeval sands,
to the African bush.
The blackness is vacant no more.

Conjuring woman
what can she do with fingertips
in the silent web-weaving of paths

for her children?
Dwelling in mythocracy,
The world of the ancients
becomes her own.

Pagan Nepantla: Searching for Identity

Abel R. Gomez

When I went to my first public pagan ritual at 16 years old, race was the furthest thing from my mind. Because Witchcraft was not something my family was familiar, much less comfortable with, my aunt Anabella agreed to go with me. As we surveyed the space, walked around altars, and watched other participants walk by, my aunt turned to me and said, "I think we're the only Latinos here." I looked at her and said, "I think you're right". At the time, I was not looking for a community that shared my culture or spoke my family's language. I was drawn powerfully to the spirituality of the Craft – connecting with the primal Elements, the old Gods, and the living forces of the natural world.

I continued to attend public rituals, which led to taking classes, organizing local pagan events, co-priestessing rituals, and eventually stepping through the gateway of initiation into the Reclaiming Tradition of the Craft. Initiation awakened something in me that I had never really thought about, the ancestors of my blood culture. During the ceremony, I was ritually connected to the Mighty Dead of the Craft, the lineage of Witches that has existed since the beginning of time. I was given a whole new set of ancestors, and yet, I came to realize that I had no real knowledge of the ancestors that I already had. Initiation shined a light on what I had seemed to ignore for most of my life. To reclaim my ancestors and my culture was yet another step in reclaiming all my parts of self.

When I look back, it seems so clear to me why I had

let go, in some sense, of strong cultural ties. As a queer person, there seemed no place for me in the Latino Catholic culture of my family. Further, as a child it seemed that nearly all the images that were available to me of Latino men were gangsters, alcoholics, or men who battered their wives. It also did not help that my mother, a daughter of immigrant parents from Nicaragua and El Salvador, disliked my father's Mexican Spanish so much that my parents rarely spoke to me in Spanish. Of course, the fact that I practiced Pagan spirituality was yet another block (or so it seemed) from connecting to my blood culture. I wonder how similar this story is to folks who identity as ethnic minorities or people of color.

Beyond stereotypes and seeming boundaries, the medicine of my initiation pushed me to seek out my blood ancestors. This call was deeper than simply wanting to put together an altar for dead relatives at Samhain, though I think that practice is also important. It was also about understanding my own story, my own history. In my sophomore year of as an undergraduate, I took a counseling class in which we read Randall Robinson's *The Debt: What America Owes to Blacks*. Within the pages of the first chapter, Randall writes a passage that would stay with me for many years, "No people can live successfully, fruitfully, triumphantly without strong memory of their past..." (Randall 27). It was after initiation that the power of these words had real meaning to me. Unless I knew my own history, unless I knew of those on whose shoulders I stand, I could not truly step into my future.

In an effort to learn my history, I joined Latina/o student organizations, engaged in conversations with family, and took classes in the Latina/o Studies department at my university. Along the way I came across *Borderlands/La Frontera: The New Mestiza* by queer feminist Xicana author Gloria Anzaldúa. Anzaldúa's later work explores the concept of nepantla, a Nahuatl word for "in between". In the preface of her co-edited anthology *This Bridge We Call Home: Radical Visions for Transformation*, Anzaldúa writes, "Transformations occur in this in-between space, an unstable, unpredictable, precarious, always-in-transition space...Nepantla es tierra desconocida, and living in this liminal zone means being in a constant state of displacement—an uncomfortable, even alarming feeling" (Anzaldúa 1). She uses nepantla to describe what it means to be in between genders, cultures, worlds, states of being, and other spaces of liminality. As I considered Anzaldúa words, I noticed that I was in states of nepantla in many places in my life. Working to embody both pride in my ancestry and the values of the Craft was one that I was just beginning to explore.

My studies in Feri Tradition continually remind me that Victor Anderson (the first Grandmaster of the tradition) would encourage his students to learn the magic of their ancestral culture. When I turned to my family to help find answers, the resounding response was that they did not exactly know where we came from, where we could trace our line to, beyond the idea that we are mixed. The word "Latino" is in some sense a nepantla word, spanning several countries and referring to various levels of indigenous, African, and European ancestry. Speaking to family revealed that I have ancestry from the Americas, Europe, and perhaps even Cuba. Where exactly I can trace my roots still seems a bit ambiguous. My ancestry appears, itself, to be in a place of nepantla.

For someone in a space of cultural nepantla, finding identity within the context of modern Paganism may be especially difficult given the fact that our traditions draw primarily from Europe. People of all backgrounds have been welcomed to the Pagan events and communities I have been a part of. At the same time, there is a difference in that the traditions, myths, and gods of non-European peoples are not often worked with in ritual, except in the case of Hindu, Sumerian, and Egyptian cultures. How do mixed people and/or people of color incorporate their ancestral culture into their pagan practice, if at all? The question becomes especially difficult when a person does not quite know where she comes from. Unlike a person who can trace his ancestry to Greece and know that his ancestors worshiped Gaia, Artemis, and Hera, one who cannot trace his ancestry will likely have a more difficult time incorporating spirituality, identity, and culture.

My own experience around this has proven challenging. My mother's side of the family is darker than my father's and I am told that through my mother's line, there was some indigenous ancestry at some point. Because my Mexican father's side of the family is light skinned, I turned out to be much lighter than many of my friends who identify as Xicano or Latino. Given this, I wonder what cultural traditions I can claim as my own. Is my ancestry too European to claim blood ties to indigenous spirituality of Mexico or Central America? Should I focus my energy on the ancestral traditions of Spain or another place in Europe? Here, again, I find myself in the place of nepantla.

I still have not found concretes answers to questions about practice and ancestry, but I have found something quite remarkable in La Virgen de Guadalupe. She, like my own ancestors, is a mix of cultures, religions, and traditions. Guadalupe appeared to an indigenous Mexican man named Juan Diego on the hill of Tepeyac in 1531, a place that was originally a shrine to the Aztec mother goddess Tonantzin. She told him that She would be a voice of the oppressed, the silenced, the ignored and fight for justice on their behalf. Though Guadalupe has become an important element of Mexican Catholicism, nearly all the symbolism of Her iconography is indigenous. She blends the political, spiritual, cultural, and ancestral threads of Mexican culture. Guadalupe is a nepantla goddess.

Even if I could not trace my ancestors very far to particular places, I know that at least some of them venerated La Virgen. Amidst the often frustrating and confusing place of neplanta, I was able to find something that could call my own, an ancestral connection to the world of spirit. Her image now plays a prominent role on my ancestor altar and throughout my home. I may never find the sort of answers I am looking for about where I come from, but perhaps the place of nepantla is a potent identity in itself. I will continue to pray, practice, and listen, and perhaps, the ancestors will reveal more along the way.

Bibliography

Anzaldúa, Gloria E. "(Un)natural Bridges, (Un)safe Spaces". *This Bridge We Call Home: Radical Visions for Transformation*. Ed. Gloria Anzaldúa and AnaLouise Keating. New York: Routledge, 2002.

Robinson, Randall. *The Debt: What America Owes to Blacks*. New York: Dutton, 2000.

The Smudge Stick

Janet Callahan

I light the bundle of sage, and smell the rich, sweet scent.

I fan the smoke, cleansing myself and the area around me of negative spirits, energy, thoughts, and feelings. I ask for health, healing, and peace for all who are here, and for all who enter our home.

For me, the scent belongs to two different places, and comes with two different sets of expectations. And most of the time, at least in my own workings, both are true.

One is the Pagan side of things. The realm of Gods and Goddesses, spirits of places near and far. A combination of fire, earth, and air cleansing the space.

The other is the Native American side of things; the stuff of powwows, and sweat lodges, and the long and colorful history of my Lakota ancestors.

Smudging happens at both Pagan events and Native American events – it is part and parcel of both. Though to be upfront, the use of the term smudge in Pagan settings is a bit questionable, because the term belongs to Native tribes. In either case, I'm clearing space with smoke from one or more plants. A tiny point of intersection between two parts of me that are both very different and startlingly similar.

Smudging is a frequent ritual at our house because we have medically complex children. We have multiple caregivers, therapists, and caseworkers coming in and out of our home every week, and the overall energetic build-up needs cleaning up much the way we sweep the floors to clear out the dirt they track in on their visits.

In the moment that I light the sage, I rarely wonder

whether I am doing a Native thing or a Pagan thing. It doesn't much matter in our house, because I am both.

For the moment, my children are both, because they are born Native, and they live in the flow of our Pagan practice and belief until they are ready to choose otherwise. It is just a part of what we do. I present it to them as something we do to cleanse our home and our energy, rather than as something that belongs to either culture. When they are bigger, this is just a small part of the conversations we will have on this subject, and many related subjects – race, privilege, generational trauma, cultural appropriation. These are such big subjects for little children, and yet a part of their everyday life, subjects they will need to understand to make sense of the world around them.

That conversation is something I can give them that my own mother could not give me. Generational trauma haunts our past, stealing our culture for generations at a time. My great grandparents attended a boarding school whose primary mission was to make them into good Americans – Christians, rather than "savage" Natives with superstitious beliefs.

The more I read, the more I realize that those running the schools understood, more than most people today, that culture and language and traditional beliefs are all one and the same – all woven together in a rich tapestry.

What they failed to understand was that they could not just strip away the Indian and make those children White.

My great-grandmother, my grandmother's stepmother, would not teach my grandmother or my mother anything traditional. I believe in her mind it wasn't safe, she was trying to shield them from the experiences she'd had, but she always told my mother it was "too hard" to learn.

So, they didn't burn sage growing up. They didn't

have access to traditional ways, language, healing, or other cultural practices. I daresay that I know more about my culture today than my grandmother does...and she lives on the reservation, on the ranch she grew up on, and has spent more than a decade working in an elementary school there, amongst children whose families run the gamut from very traditional to not at all traditional.

In some respects, this returning to traditional ways, no matter how I arrived here, is a victory.

Burning herbs for spiritual purposes has a long history among many cultures – not just Pagan or Native American. The question of "smudging" in Pagan groups, and whether that counts as cultural appropriation doesn't come up all that often, probably because the idea (if not the specific herbs) is one that many cultures share.

Even within Native cultures (and there are many of them), there are differences in how smudging is done – some use shells, some believe the spirit of the water the shell embodies clashes with the fire of burning sage. Some use other herbs. Some use sage to clear and sweet grass to bring in clean energy. Some use white sage, some use desert sage and some use something else entirely.

Not that there aren't issues of appropriation in the Pagan community, mind you. I am cautious about participating in some events because I want to avoid those issues. I honor both my culture of birth and my current faith by using discretion in whom I circle with. Maybe I judge too harshly, but the history of my people shows me that I need to be aware of who I trust, and what their intentions are.

But all in all, I'm ok with this overlap – a solid point of connection between two parts of my soul is a good thing, and makes the attempts at balancing those two parts a little easier. Smudging, and its counterparts in many different cultures, gives me a starting point when I have to discuss other issues of cultural appropriation in the Pagan community.

And so, I teach all of it to my little ones this way. Sage is a way to clean our energy – a way to take our prayers and our intentions to the Gods – a little housekeeping chore, like doing the dishes. We use a shell to hold the sage. We use a modern source of fire (a cigarette lighter – my grandmother points out that us Indians have always been resourceful people, using everything available, and if our ancestors had Bic lighters, they surely would have used them, because they weren't stupid). Most days we just use our hands to direct the smoke, though some days a fan made of feathers seems more appropriate.

Many of my Native friends and family use fans made with feathers from an eagle or hawk when smudging. Several years ago, I bought a beautiful fan at a powwow that used bright blue, red, and green macaw feathers.

So I'm not quite traditional.

It's ok. I think my ancestors would think so too.

Circle of Understanding

Clio Ajana

"Being loving - you treat yourself well -
you don't allow yourself to be treated badly,
 to put bad things into your body, to be spoken to badly.
 - Chandra
(Dr. Bailey on *Grey's Anatomy*)

"Find the ones who need you to sing to, for them, in the world."
 David Citino, March 17, 2000 - OSU Commencement address poem

The early hours of the morning, the time when night remains wrapped in dark velvet, marks an invisible journey of sorts. It is not yet dawn, when tendrils of light will bring another day, with its worries, joys and reality. It is a time of promises, of burgeoning hopes, of pregnant silence. It is my favorite time of the day. There is no end and no beginning at this time of the night. Dawn, with its light-filled presence, announces the fixed, the finite. Night resembles the unconscious, the lack of the known, the land of mystery.

It is just past four in the morning. The birds have not awakened or stirred from their nests on the grape vines remains that cling outside my window. If I leave the light on accidentally at night, with the blinds open, they are restless and squeak loudly. I have learned to close my blinds to the northwest and southwest windows in the living room. The stillness pierces my sleep-deprived brain. My body is in that split-state familiar to parents of young children, college students during exam week, and truckers pulling double shifts. My muscles have gone beyond their limits, yet my brain spins even faster.

I choose to cast a Circle of Understanding. My writing, like my spiritual life, is a journey that has taken me far from my origins. Four in the morning is the hour of aloneness, of recalling journeys past, and of understanding the fears hidden in the heart. I place four tall glass candles in a circle: yellow, red, blue and green for the elements of air, fire, water and earth. I open myself up to the Divine, to allow myself to be a vessel, an ambassador to communicate how spiritual change happens in the most unlikely of circumstances. I ask for creative help from above. I ask for protection from below to explore the ebbs and flows of a process that both heals and cleanses me.

I enter the circle, as I enter a book, with questions, with unfulfilled and unknown desires. It is the night before my defense, before I must submit an essay that defines the twenty books that have impacted my life as a writer, and my time in the Creative Writing Program at the University of Minnesota.

Writing is ritual. Ritual is writing. Until now, I had not asked for creative help in a circle. Tiredness leaked from my body.

I call upon my ancestors: my father, his mother, and the spirits of the storytellers, missionaries and preachers who make up my line.

What needs to die?

The words come to me in haze.

What needs to live?

Images of works that touch my soul flood my mind, Patricia Weaver Francisco's memoir of rape, *Telling*, Joan Didion's memoir of loss, *The Year of Magical Thinking*, and Lynn Freed's memoir of growth, *Reading, Writing and Leaving Home*.

Home. Think of home. Spirituality. Death.

I pick up a purple ink pen and yellow pad from the eastern edge of the circle, where they lay on a yellow cloth, covering the east altar. I leave my writing supplies in the east, because that direction represents the element of air, communication and trust. I need to trust to have faith in the Gods. Trust forms the foundation of my writing.

I write about my fears, the lack of trust that I would, like a character from Didion's work, make it over the Sierras before the snow falls. I write about how death and my spiritual choices change my life between my first year in the program and my last year in the program.

Grief.

The most stunning moment in my writing is the memory of when I am in a waiting room, as my aunt lies in a coma, footsteps away. A surgeon arrives to tell another family, an Arab family, how their loved one lives but will not be the same again. The wails of the wife, dressed in blue, haunt me then and now. I am tied to their grief, then and now, because I am human. Whether Christian, Jew or pagan, I am human and I grieve with those who experience loss.

Sadness.

I recall how I choose not to use this scene, because it does not connect with what I consider to be my spiritual journey at that time. Now, I see that the grief and loss are just as real now, a part of the circle now, as the wails are in my mind.

Balance.

I write peace and balance. Ritual provides both for me. I am awake before dawn, when no one moves in this large early twentieth century mansion, to restore peace to my soul.

Help me to find the words.

The pen moves, slowly, then more quickly. The spirits speak. I listen. The Gods advise. I listen.

Include food in the final draft.

They remind me that a part of my spiritual home is one where food, its presence and its preparation have great meaning.

Delete the jargon.
I cross out the terms that do not fit the essay's style.
Community. Family. Wholeness.

My reason for casting circle is the same reason I sit in circle: I am at home. This is my community, my family. In writing, the program provides a community of writing. In faith, the lodge is my family of faith. I find my voice in the lodge and with the Gods, just as I find my writing voice in the community of writers in the creative writing program.

Home.

In circle, my writing wrestles with the question of conversion. The ritual answers the larger questions: Why did I leave Christianity for Judaism? *To find a spiritual home.*

Why did I embrace Hellenic Orthodox? *It is a better fit for me overall as a spiritual home, both for my past as a single, straight woman and my present as a lesbian witch.* Is this really the last time? *Yes. There is enough to last a lifetime here.*

I hear the Gods and my ancestors around me.

The voice you have now is not the voice you had before. Learn. Trust. Grow.

You are never alone.

I remain seated in the Circle of Understanding, giving thanks for allowing me to learn how to share what is in my soul with others. When I ask if there is anything more I need to know, I feel a tug downward on my left side. I feel grounded, centered and ready to give. I rise, grateful for the help I have received for my creative endeavors. In each direction, north, west, south and east, I bid farewell to those who came. I blow out the candles and leave the circle. Let me find the ones who need the voice only I can bring to the page. Let the writing begin, again. It is five fifteen. Dawn is coming.

Finding Your Place:
My Socio-Emotional-Political Practice

Crystal Blanton

Being who I am is a very important piece to my spiritual self. Identifying the various parts that make up who I am today is one of the most spiritual acts I can do. For these reasons, I have chosen to honor the various parts that make up the whole me, and trying to incorporate them equally into my daily practice of walking this path.

Embracing being a Black woman is not just about cultural identity, it connects me to a history that is rich in power and strong in resilience. I have a strong belief that the way that people use the word resilience today, especially referring to children and people, is not accurate. Resilience to me does not mean that a person reverts back to what he or she was prior to their experience. Resilience instead means that the impact of circumstances in life have the ability to forever change our perspectives and experiences in life, and yet we are able to rise above the often debilitating changes in life, despite the circumstances. This theme has been a strong part of my life, not just as a Black person, but also as a woman, and a lower-middle class mother.

I was born out of the oppressive past of my ancestors, and the restrictions of an often unempathetic society, to become a strong woman of conviction in my ethical, spiritual and professional life. I have been asked in the past why I have to mention that I am Black, and in reality, part of it is because I am proud, and also because it is one of the most impactful factors of my experience on my daily walk.

It is not something to be afraid of, or to shy away from, or to forget; being Black is a direct connection to the path of my ancestors, and in experiencing the collective history of generations before me. Referring to my Blackness is not a statement of victimization, and it is not meant to make non-Black people feel uncomfortable, guilty, or unimportant.

I tend to believe that the eclectic style of my practice reflects that eclectic style of my ancestry, and of my history. The ability to integrate many different aspects and variables of life is an adaptation necessary in our history, and has become a conditioned skill for African American people. Survival often meant, and means today, having the ability to integrate the expectations of our surroundings while also staying true to our personal convictions. This is a challenging balance, the balancing of two sets of expectations, and yet it is one that we have practiced for centuries. And the beauty of this balance allows me the flexibility to honor the social, emotional and political experiences I am having, and make that a part of my religious practice.

"Standing in my place of power,
I am walking a path of empowerment within myself,
Spreading healing to the pieces of the world in which I can reach,
In actions that speak of a future blessed by spirit,
And in honor of the Gods of all time.

On the shoulders of millions I stand,
On the path to greatness I am creating,
A light on the opportunities of tomorrow I am shining,
So that I may see my path towards actualization,
And show my children the road to themselves."

And thus I feel this is one of the most important pieces to the puzzle; integrating history, culture and spirituality into practice. It wasn't until I started to understand the necessity of doing this that I was able to connect to an authentic path. I couldn't see the disconnect between my cultural self, my sociopolitical self and my spiritual self until I started to integrate them together, making for a whole practice that reached every side of my being. I had passed the place in my personal growth where I could see all those pieces of myself as separate, and instead understood that they were all the eclectic pieces to my integrated soul.

Part of the personal milestone I have come to understand is that I am more powerful when I am working towards the complete picture of who I am in the world. As with magic, all things are connected and my inability to make the conscious connection between the social, political, cultural, and emotional foundations only hampered my magic from flowing naturally.

Using the power of my energy to enhance change in the world would require pulling energy from all parts of myself and channel it into the manifestation I am hoping to create. It is with this energy that I am willing change that will support a better life for myself, my family, and the society that I live within. The cultural capital that I have to aid in this arena, different than some others, would be the very unique parts of my ancestry, culturally oppressive past, and social work present. I have come to believe that this collective approach to spirituality is actually the road back to myself; it is the past, present and future evolution of my people.

This is how I have come to embrace Wiccan spirituality inside of my sense of a culturally colored context. It is within the purview of the Gods to do this work, and to be one spiritual being, historical past and a future of infinite possibilities combined. It is not just about the Gods that I chose to work with, as many of Pagans of color are challenged with the strong eurocentric concept of deities, but it is also about the work and energy that directly impacts the social construct of people of color in today's society.

And now the how.... How does this work? It is the action and the practice, the mundane and the magical, the spoken word and the prayer.

The combination of action in the physical world to enhance the needs of a just society is a direct part of my spiritual practice. It is not just about what I do at the altar, but also what I do within society. You see, I believe that the Gods use us to do their work on this plane. We become the mouthpieces, the hands, and the feet of the Gods within this world. So when I am fighting for funding for children in urban schools, or advocating for mental health services, food, shelter, or doing counseling with a child, I am doing the work of the Gods. It is directly linked with my connection to the divine, and my place in the world.

And then there is the spiritual practice, communing with the divine in which I serve and the ancestors that came before me. When in ritual, I do not separate my magic from my mundane mission, from my sociopolitical advocacy. All those things are connected, and the Gods understand that position more than we know, they are the ones that put me right here, right now.

So many of my workings include honoring justice and equality, giving thanks for the ancestors and Mighty Dead that came before me, social justice advocacy and lending power to create change, and for clarity for us all to create change together. These are the things I speak to the gods about. I pray for those who are unjustly caught in a cycle of the unjust racial caste system of mass incarceration, and the new Jim Crow laws, or for those families that have lost their children to racial profiling and racial injustice. I do workings for the poor, and for the homeless. I make it my spiritual business to be aware of the sociopolitical climate of injustice happening to the disenfranchised here in America, and then I commune with the Gods.

"In this circle of mind and breath
I bring love to the ancestors that suffered in death
by the chains of slavery and bound by fear
Healing from past bondage is brought near,
Energy for closure,
of what you had to endure,
I honor your pain as your sacrifice for my today
In gratitude I celebrate you for all the words you were not able to say,
I hear those words in the building of my soul,
And honor the age old wisdom of the slaves often untold.
With peace I send this message, with love I send healing,
With hope we move forward into our true spiritual being."

And all of my workings are not about the world outside of my home. It is introspective work about breaking the bonds of historical trauma from my ancestral history, and transgenerational healing. I also include my family in this, and the ability to grow beyond the boundaries of society, to grow to a place of self actualization beyond the box of others expectations. I believe that one of the biggest jobs I have as a parent is to make sure that my children understand that they are not limited by the world's understanding of cultural capital and what they have to give to the world. Society will not always understand what they have to give, and only they can decide what that is. The misguided concept of a life that is based on egalitarian views is not the whole of the picture and I want my children to understand that, so that they can make their decisions on who they are in the world. Then they can create magic.

"I weave together these threads, to symbolize the intertwining magic that connects me to myself. A representation of divine knowledge that is one part ancestral wisdom, one part divine knowledge and one part wisdom from my experiences on

this plane."

(weave three different strands together, preferably different colors to distinguish between the different parts of the collective. Read the following while weaving the threads together)
"Weaving wisdom
Three parts to one
Collective togetherness
Within my body, be it done
As I will it, it is so"
This thread can be used in a multitude of ways. One of my suggestions would be to tie it around the outside of a 7 day pillar candle and light the candle when invoking your collective wisdom.

The magic of our collective history and our present makes for an exceptionally powerful foundation for using our past and our present to create our future. This type of magic goes beyond the magic we read about in the 101 books about love, and luck. It is a deeper, ancestral, cultural, emotional, political, and social magic that can only come from those who are willing to break down the walls that compartmentalize their lives and trail a path as a person that walks with the past, present and future. I believe it is the way of our people to do this, it is how we have survived and will continue to survive, beyond the legacy of trauma we have been pained with through our history.

And I do believe this is one of the imperative pieces to building a society of equality for those to come after us.

Healing in the Dark of Injustice

(a working written after the verdict of the Trayvon Martin trial, for his family and those families who have lost a loved one to social injustice)
As the water flows to the sea, let the tears of grief release the sorrow in your heart.

As the earth is soft beneath your feet, let the healing powers of the earth care for your pain.

As the air brushes across your check, let whispers of love comfort the child now beyond our mortal reach.

As the fire breeds heat that brings about transformation, let the spark of justice rise like the phoenix to change this broken system.

As the spirits of the Gods live within our flesh, the vision of hope lives within our path. Let it be known that we are all the messengers of love, empowered with the mission of righteous equality. As grief transforms into fuel, fuel is a means to justice, justice becomes the road to enlightenment.

Tonight we pray for healing love. Tomorrow we fight for justice…. for all.

Blessings onto the parents of the lost.

Blessings onto a community in grief.

Blessings onto a society that is rooted in confusion and bound by fear.

Blessings onto the change agents that fight for a future that is not guaranteed.

May this collective rage encourage right action that will lead to peace within our souls.

May it be so.

Delphian Whispers

Pablo Vazquez III

Through the golden wings of Nike
I soar through the rocky trails
Roughly coated in an ancient fog
There mine misted eyes are sewn
A cosmic soul sundered by glory

Lost in obsidian visions
You lie on the distant dark horizon
Eyes that dance like ghostly embers
Flickering to the tune of elder songs
A Botticelli in Artemisian clothes

The stars steal away my shadowed whispers
Sin-eaters from the supernovas
A silent confession to Helios delivered
A brazen demand before the mystic heavens
To behold a boundless aurora

Let the templed mountains shake
Filled with awe of heart-born majesty
Kali clears the ballroom battlefields
Pirouetting over corpses of the old world
Our timeless tango of flawless love

My Love of Serpents

Rt. Rev. Anniitra Ravenmoon

Sister Serpents of the Wheel
Never ending
I am Yours
As you hold me and wear me,
Empower yourself with the
Beauty that surrounds you

I don't actually know when I started to love serpents.

I was raised in a family that was/is anti-snake/serpent. Never thought I would be so rebellious! To me the snake represents our ancient primordial mother.

When I was trying to find myself in the Baptist church, all I heard was that we have been doomed because a snake told Eve to eat from a forbidden tree. I started being more curious about them when my goddess spirituality seemed to honor them in a different way. New revelations just opened right and left for me. There was no way I could understand why some cultures and faiths, although not many, regard serpent as a mean, demonic animal. It was a revelation to see this beautiful animal that represents rebirth, change, growth, and sacred movement. To me, the snake/serpent was/ is a matrix for us all to regenerate ourselves with transformation, and renewal. "Divine Serpent" reminds me of the beautiful moves and undulations of our Kundalini. I have a snake vertebrae necklace, and a shedded rattle that I place on my altar when honoring our Dark Moon.

I thought I would also honor her by this beautiful artwork, and piece that I wear very proudly, that sometimes turns Christians (some of them) away because they're afraid of the snake. I better say that not all Christians are afraid of snakes, but at the time I was attending the Christian church, they thought snakes were taboo. So this is my honoring to the divine serpent.

The Passion and Soul of Serpentinology

Along with my Serpentinology (That's my made up word) serpent jewelry, I also like to dance using serpent movements.

I have been teaching North African dance since 1980; North Africa is Egypt. Bellydance comes from Africa, but up until recently, you would not hear the word African in relation to bellydance. When I first started dancing in 1977, you could count the black women on one hand that I saw. Back then they only knew that it came from Egypt, but as time went on, we came to associate with Egypt as North African, and this art form as a cultural family dance. This same dance called belly dance by Europeans.

My slow, liquid moves are my admiration, and honoring to the "Sacred Serpent". I want to share with you some of my liquid 'Serpentinology Moves".

Music To Use: Use slow, slow, liquid music, such as: "Reality of a dreamer by Mythos."

~Hands of Spiraling serpents~ Descent of hands in a slow spiral/or S to
Frame lower body.
Flow into hip movements, with my "Ravenluscious" waves (serpent S), with descent of serpentine hands, framing the hips. (This looks like your hips moving slow, with your hands also flowing like an S")
~Serpentinology Finger curls~ softly closed, then open slowly with wave of fingers
Dives~ making slow diving motions downwards with fingers, then whole hand,
Ascent to upper body, and overhead with Cartwheels.

The Passion And Soul of Our Primordial Mother

"Yes, I am black! and radiant--"
The eyes of many morning suns
Have pierced my skin, and now I shine
Black light before the dawn."
(Adapted from book Song of Songs by Marcia Falk)

It doesn't matter who you are, or what color you are: we ALL have an African Queen as our primordial, ancestral mother. Our Ancient African mothers used dance as a lifeline of communication, and a tool for various celebrations.

Our African Mothers were revered for their beautiful luscious hips, and their full beautiful lips. We were taught to hide the natural, rhythmic sway of our luscious hips. Our lips were once made fun of, but now are sought after. Our Mother Africa has given birth to so many different styles of dance and cultures. Our African ancestral mothers balanced babies on one hip, and walked with a sway, while balancing a water jug on their heads. We come from
A long line of African Queens!!

Quinquatrus

Clio Ajana

As an African-American woman, I am proud to worship as I choose: I worship the Greek, Roman and Egyptian gods. We honor the ancestors and look to them, as well as the gods, for guidance and strength. While we follow the general cycle, known as the 'Wheel of the Year', with a few additional sabbats: Quinquatrus, the sabbat marking the campaign season. Until a few years ago, it was not my favorite sabbat. I had not embraced my warrior nature, the harsh side of myself that would be necessary to continue along the path of a witch. The warrior side is what sustains me as a person of color. Often I am the only person of color in a ritual or at a pagan gathering in my local area.

One particular Quinquatrus cemented my desire to stand tall and proud as the Pagan person of color that I am. As a season, Quinquatrus falls in the twilight period between winter and spring. The February sabbat of Brunalia concludes a month earlier; the Vernalia sabbat hailing the return of Persephone and a celebration of the Spring Equinox is a week or so later. Six in the evening on a quiet rainy March Saturday in St. Paul can be dreary, even with a partly visible moon. The bare US Bank parking lot across the street from the Sacred Paths Community Center and the slow foot traffic into the corner liquor store said it all. The community center is now gone, but that day reminded me that one can never step down from the reality of race and skin color in a primarily white community.

The distinct smell of Nag Champa and the sound of brass bells permeated the room as I opened the heavy glass door.

"Are you with Our Lady of Celestial Fire?" the dark haired woman, dressed in a flourescent orange sweater and blue jeans, looked closer to fifteen than the twenty-five she probably was, looked upheld a place in her book and nudged her shoulder towards the back. I nodded. She looked new.

"Set up's back there. It's twenty-five an hour now."

"Sure. Is it okay to pay at the end?"

"Absolutely. Susan will be in later to collect." She smiled as though relieved not to have to handle money. Some of the volunteers at this center were like that.

"I'm Joan, in case you need anything."

I chuckled and picked up the heavy bag of ritual papers, food and clothing. Joan was already back into her book by the time I looked up again.

The room, with collage of blue carpet samples, bare spots in the corners, five misshapen tables, and a late 90s microwave stand, reminded me more of my mother's basement or an antique shop. Our group came for convenience, not the atmosphere: it was on a bus line.

Tonight I would state my intentions before the Gods, for the remainder of the year. What would I manifest in my life? What would I nurture? What would I fight to build in my life? Like a warrior, I wore full gear: a white peplos or toga, sewn from crisp white linen bed sheets, a red sash, a set of braided cords (scarlet, black, silver, gold and white), a measure of rope, an athame and brown leather sandals with white seashells. Now, at my fifth Quinquatrus, I was finally campaigning for a change in my own life on paper, in prayer and into action. My writing addressed the harder questions that I hadn't dared to do five years ago: infertility, grief and a final spiritual resting place. I needed more of a challenge in the classroom and less of the gypsy existence of adjunct life. Spiritual questions were no longer about my connection to the Gods or why their existence in my life mattered: I was in the driver's seat of my own life, where the entrance to the mysteries was a reality, not an afterthought.

Perhaps five or six new people might show up. But the rain earlier and the musky, funky Saturday evening, promised just our group, pilgrims in prayer and devotion to our Gods, enjoying the last bits of winter before spring.

I had to find the plug in for the crockpot that someone would inevitably bring, so I asked Joan when she came back to see if I had everything I needed in the room.

"Sure, we have the cord here," she said, pointing to a tangled mess of one table, four chairs and a thin yellow extension cord that wound through it all.

"Thanks. Do you want to come to ritual?" I asked. It was a polite enquiry.

"Sure. I've always wanted to know more about Orisha."

I tried not to raise my eyebrows too much. Here I am, dressed in a white toga with red stola, setting up a Hellenistic ritual that has been advertised in their store. I wondered, did this woman not read? Our group's name "Our Lady of Celestial Fire" should have been a clue.

"Ummm..." Silence. I don't know what to say. What can I say in the face of ignorance?

" Hey, don't you teach that? Haven't I seen you giving classes in Orisha here at the Center before?"

And there it was. The moment I dreaded. As a black Pagan, my skin color and dark brown eyes stand out in this northern land of white skins, pink tones, blond or red hair and light colored eyes. *Gee, I guess you all look alike.* It was never said, but that was the tone.

"No. I'm Hellenic Alexandrian. That's all I've done."

I let my frustration linger in the silence. She paused, with the awkwardness common in these exchanges. Do I save this woman or not? I wonder. It was a common situation in the land of Minnesota nice: be polite and ignore the clear inference that there were so few Pagans of color that we must all look alike or worse, be the same person. The other alternative was to let out the anger and rage towards all who lived in this land and could not see me for who I am.

"Oh, okay." Joan doesn't flinch from my stare, but rocks back and forth on her feet, her hair dangling at an odd angle.

"You probably met me at Pagan Pride last year." I toss her a nudge.

It's a sabbat. I'm feeling generous. As a priestess, I am supposed to teach through example. Perhaps she will learn.

She grabs onto my words, a sigh of relief in her eyes.

"Yeah. That's it." She smiled and walked back to the front.

An hour later, as we began chanting our opening prayer, the *Dialexis a Stauros*, I caught a glimpse of dark hair and a bright orange shirt off to the right side. Joan's body swayed to an invisible rhythm. By the middle part of ritual, the orange had disappeared. *Another one bites the dust*, I thought.

On my way out, I saw her again, fingers in book, as she stood by the cash register.

"So, did you like ritual?"

"I couldn't stay. I liked that sing song part at first, but I had to work in the basement." She shrugged as though she had no choice in the matter.

"The fridge was dirty, and it was my turn..." Her voice trailed off.

"Maybe next time." I smiled and left.

I wanted to tell her about my past, before I found my true home in Paganism. I wanted her to see me as more than just a freak, an anomaly in the land of pale whiteness. I was just like her. I sought the spiritual home that would fulfill me. I didn't find it with the Christian God for 19 years. I didn't find it with the Jewish God for 18 years. I found it within the call from the Gods as a Pagan.

Only in Christianity was skin color not an issue. I wanted to ask her: why do you presume that black skin means we only practice African tradition? Why do we, the pagans of color, remain restricted to a box that can be easily identified and marked? Why do you stare when we show up as though we were lost on the way to someplace else? I wanted to ask her in the name of every white Pagan stare and questioning eyes each time I put on my robe and cords, each time I cast a circle, each time I draw down, each time I lead a ritual. The answers were memorized now: no, I'm not crazy. No, I am not any less black, any less human because I do not practice African tradition. Yes, I am offended by your willful ignorance, by your need to ask these questions, and by my need to be polite and silent in the land of paleness and presumptions.

West in East

Yutaka Furuki

Young Japanese Magician

I still remember the first day when I was drawn to Western Magic. I was a teenager; the snow was falling on that cold day when I went to a large bookstore where I found a book of Magic. Fortunately it was a real good book by W. E. Butler titled in Japanese as "Trainings of Magic", which was actually the translation of "Apprenticed to Magic". I didn't know there was systematic training, or discipline in Western Magic, and that was a real surprise for a Japanese kid at that time. I was also fascinated by the way the trainings lead practitioners to hidden dimension, and the way Quabalah was employed for interpreting the universe. I started to do exercises everyday following the instructions of the book.

In the early 90`s there were only several dozen practical Western Magical books published in Japanese language. It would be 10 more years before publications of reputable Wiccan titles were available. For the last thirty years, I think that many people interested in Western traditions in Japan got involved with Golden Dawn related magic; in these fifteen or twenty years Wiccan practice also became popular. I was also an aspiring teen practitioner of Hermetic Magic. Breathing exercise and meditations became my pleasure, giving me a sense of being as I am, in moments of bliss. I enjoyed the contrast between mundane activity in the day as student and quiet meditations in the night. While I was having a normal school life with studying and sports, there was no one who showed understanding of my most exciting and profound hobby.

In Japan almost no one knew there were serious Magicians, Witches and Pagans that were handing down traditions in the West. I was a little frustrated that no one had even a slight glimpse of what the magic was about.

At the time there were a few Japanese magical orders lead by Japanese Adepts. Some of them were from magical orders of western countries or students of older generation magicians in Japan. There was no Internet at the time, no deeper information on practice; we all had to make some effort to find people who were really practicing magic. I made contacts with a few orders and decided to join one of them.

The order's education system was great for me. It was carefully designed in accordance with the basic structure of traditional Hermetic magic (and more). In the order I had magical friends and all of them were older than me. I finally had a place to breath, a place where I could talk about magic, which had been my passion. Many members were university students, or young women or men in their early 20`s; all of them were Japanese. Monthly gathering where we had rituals, experiments and discussion usually ended the next morning, or sometimes the next afternoon. I did magical training five or six days a week. I spent more than 2 hours every day just training on magic in my younger days. If I read magical books on such a schedule, my life was full of magical stuff.

Becoming a Minority

After some time I became a university student and kept training in the order. I advanced some in the order, and daily works became more subtle and fascinating. I had experienced many rituals, and had frequent lucid dreams and synchronicity. My etheric sense was developed and strengthened in energy and auric work. I was still a novice but my personality was firmly centered in magical personality; I felt I could come back to who I was most when I was wearing my black robe, visualizing pentagrams, or invoking a deity in the circle. Because I felt a sense of purification and the flow of the subtle energy each time I did the practice, it became my second nature. I experienced most profound moments when I was doing these magical exercises. It was the moment my inner most self fully awaked into the light.

There were no people in the university who had an understanding on magical subjects. It was a very rare coincidence to have a certain degree of understanding in Western Magic and Paganism in Japan. There was almost no chance you can find a practicing magician or Pagan among your friends at the time. The situation seems to be slowly changing now for new generations of magicians and witches who are holding workshops, developing social networks and publishing magical literatures. The majority of average Japanese people still do not know what these Western disciplines are. This simply means that you become a cultural minority in the country if you are practicing Western mysteries. I think all people uphold their most meaningful belief in any society and such beliefs are usually apparent to any observer. In other words, usually most people in any society believe in something that other member of the society can understand. If a young person believes in the contemporary culture, older people will recognize it, even if they do not really like it. In my case, this was magical practices and philosophies from the West. My most important possession was practices and experiences of magic, and an inner realization that magic brought to me. But I could not express that feeling, both in private and public, when not many people have a real understanding of it. Practicing spirituality, as a Magician or Pagan, may look odd to the average person, even in Western countries, if they lack true understanding of them, but in Japan the chances are slimmer to see a person who really understand the subject.

I have not felt strange when robed, holding a dagger, and intoning Hebrew names in preparation for invoking a Greek goddess. I am black haired and black eyed, and almost everyone around here shares the same appearance. And since I have not lived in Western countries, except for relative short periods, and have not lived in the Western magical community without the aid of the Internet, I have not faced the situation that I am a racial minority in a white magical community. I just liked what practices of Western magical faith brought to me, such as perception, control and mastery of self, and awareness to the world. What I felt frustrated with here was that magic and Paganisms are unrecognized, or even among the people who claim themselves as practitioners of such systems, they are often misunderstood, simply for the lack of enough information.

I fortunately could read English books on topics of magic, Paganism, Heathenry and Druidry to obtain more information than Japanese magical publishers could provide. Still many important titles on Magic and Paganism are not translated into Japanese, so I had to read English books more than Japanese ones. Such reading environment (access to wealth of magical books) may not be not readily possible for every Japanese magician or witch. Fortunately, this situation has become better in general because of improvements in Japanese people's language skills, the improvement in translation devices and cheaper digital books. I think reading cultivates worldview, opinions and many things in your character. Studying different disciplines and listening to different points of view are essential to the development of your own personal take on magical perception. Here I am a minority in Japanese society where probably only small numbers of people have enough background or frameworks of Western magic and western folk beliefs (Of course there are exceptions and the situation has now started to change). At the same time, I am far away from these Western countries by location, mother tongue, history, culture, blood and environment. It is almost inevitable to be a minority in Japanese culture if you pursue practices and faiths of magical or Pagan systems as your main belief, which I am accepting as it is.

However, Magic is ultimately not something you should explain or show others, but you feel it within from the depth of your existence, and you are able to touch the deepest mysteries without drawing attention from anyone around you. The fact that everything is magic to a magician confirms that the practice of magic is always possible no matter where you are and no matter what you are doing. Apart from theatrical gestures, incantation, magical props and symbolic divination, the real practice of Magic would not always be recognized as magic by casual observers. Attaining to a certain level of understanding the mysteries and making it on your own distinguishes you from the non-initiate, and I conceive that each initiate is loosely connected by the knowledge, practice and identity in similar discipline. That can be seen as something timeless and nearly global; especially in recent years of growing network through the Internet, and easier access to the older literatures.

Finding a Path of Norse

I have been taking a more untrodden path among Western spirituality for the Japanese circumstance these years: I am walking a way of the Northern Tradition in Japan. Originally I was also in an Armanen Runic order in early 90`s for short period. I was fascinated by worldview of Northern myth and spent time to figure out what the Runes meant. During my time in the Western magical order, I continued to read Edda and felt an affinity with the Northern Deities. One time when I was doing intensive dream work in the order, my dream body was projected out of the physical body and it was uncontrollable. Suddenly the dream body felt a sense of rising and spinning automatically that only made me dizzy. I could not control the movements of body in the dream plane at that phase of my development, later I started to learn how to control the dream body. I instinctively called for help from my most adored deity, which was Odin. I shouted the name Odin loud in the dream, then immediately I was released from the whirling, and I found I could come back to my bed. My natural faith to Odin seemed to make him my primal deity, or patron god as it could be said in the Pagan community.

Many years have passed and now my ritual room is decorated with various Northern symbols. On the altar, a statue of Odin, images of Thor and Freyr, ritual hammer, horn and gandr (wand), and runic staves are placed. A flag of raven and carving of Thor`s hammer are hanged on the wall. Although I am genetically a Japanese man, when I do daily training or perform rituals of the Runes and Germanic faith, I feel I am a priest of Germanic tradition. No one here may understand what I am doing, but I also believe that any spirituality is not something you should have to explain to anyone; rather it should be felt from the depth of your heart. I have never heard of a Japanese woman or man doing Germanic traditions as her/his primal discipline except the one Japanese man who had been running a Runic order in Japan many years ago. So far, I might be alone in this way in Japan (as long as I know), but I am not alone internationally. I belong to a couple of Runic and Northern related organization in the United States because of doing their training programs and undergoing initiation into the Germanic way. Although the distant learning would never be substitute for direct oral teaching, I believe sincere practice and study would fill the gap if you have real passion. After all, you must be your own scholar and priest when it comes to walking the heathen way or anything else. Eventually, true initiation starts from within, so it`s just up to each practitioner no matter where she/he is living. Mysteries or Runes must be taken by one`s own self, which cannot be given from someone else.

Germanic tradition for Japanese

In these three years of practice I found many similarities between Germanic mysteries with Japanese spirituality. It was as though I was given chances to review my own culture through the lens of Germanic spirituality. There are surely differences between these two cultures, but a lot of common ethoses are seen in both systems and cultures. For example, the cosmology of both cultures is mythically similar. In Germanic myth, universe is ruled by Aesirs, divine tribe of Asgard. Japanese Myth also tells that the whole world is governed by the tribe of Kami of the firmament (Amatsu Kami). Both myths have another god tribe of the earth that takes balance: Vanirs and group of Kami on the earth (Kunitsu Kami). Most sacred places are imagined as the highest place in the sky in both culture, and the country of humans are placed in the center of the whole universe. In the central place, we humans are bestowed inherent divinity from gods of the sky as both myths tell us. Such realization of beliefs of divinity in man is a strong common message that both cultures can bring. Japanese native tradition is called Shinto, which means "Way of Kami" or "Way as Kami". Germanic folk beliefs are called Asatru, "Truth" or "Loyalty" to "Aesir". Both words and concepts are indicating that we are able to walk the way, which reflects sacred divinities in this living body and in this world.

One common element in both Germanic and Japanese traditions is the strong emphasis on the warriorship. Gods of Asgard and Vanaheim are all soldiers no matter how their nature is, and Odin is also the chief commander of the entire troop. He is called father of all, and also the father of victory. In Saga literatures motif of noble heroism and courage is repeated again and again. They respected acts of honor more than anything. In the Nine Noble Virtue of Asatru movement, courage, honor and discipline are listed in there as important virtues. In Japanese Samurai soldier`s culture these same traits are held as ideals and practiced by the Samurai. You can find the spiritual background of the Samurai mentality partly in spirit of Zen. It is accepted in Samurai families for its discipline and awareness is effective way to be focused and be trained as a proficient soldier when it comes to battle. Daisetz Suzuki wrote "Zen discipline is simple, direct, self-reliant, self-denying, and this ascetic tendency goes well with the fighting spirit."(Zen and Japanese Culture, 2005)

Zen is not a way of thinking, rather it is the way the practitioner lives his life with full mindfulness, and with discipline. The Germanic culture is also characterized by straightness and discipline. Studying and following Germanic ways led me back to finding my own roots again. As Germanic and Japanese ways have some similarities in themselves, I do not feel practicing Germanic spiritualities is conflicting with my inborn being. Rather it is a process of fresh findings to me. That is the way leading far to the North but somehow taking me back to my own feet as Japanese.

I have been researching Japanese traditions. In the beginning I was asked by American occultists about Japanese spirituality and I saw undeniable common elements between them. First I found parallel between magical practice of Runes have similarity with esoteric Buddhist`s framework. Both of them classify the total of existence into the three comparable units; breath (imagination), words and body. It is no surprise because the both cultures have same Indo-European root. The emphasis on ritual incantation (e.g. Galdor and Mantra in each culture) is similar as well. The ritualistic way of singing sutra was imported to Japan more than a thousand years ago, still influencing Japanese traditional styles of singing. Comparing it with runic chants is more than interesting.

There are good reason that we Japanese resonate with the Northern religion and magic. Indeed, many heathens are interested in Shinto belief, doctrine, history and structure, for they think heathenry has some similarity with Shinto. Some would say I should pursue Shinto or Buddhism because they are art of my heritage. That would be a reasonable and serious opinion, and my answer to it would be both yes and no. I also adore Kami of Japan and respect what the Buddhism brings to the practitioners. But my primal interest is firmly centered in Western mysteries. Conversely, there are many foreigners studying and practicing Japanese traditions. We never feel it`s funny, rather we deeply respect and appreciate that they are reaching the heart of our own root, sometimes more closely than we could do.

My research and training continues. That is my personal quest into divinity, which will never end. I practice the Runes and Heathenry as my primal discipline because they resonate in my heart and I adore the Northern deities. Advanced rune practitioners have been working on their time, with their place, with their own way to preserve the runic knowledge in forms of inscriptions, literatures and the practice of Galdor and Seidr. Now I am seeking a way to somehow share acceptable runic knowledge with Japanese people who have ears listening to the Norse way.

The Long Quest for the Goddess

Leslie Brooks

I am mixed Nigerian/American White: My mother was white and my father is from Nigeria; I was raised solely by my mother. It was difficult for her, raising me by herself as well as the stress of raising a child clearly having a different skin color than her. She raised me within Christianity because it was something she thought was right.

A couple years passed within the Christian Church and she did not find the peace she wanted or needed. They frowned upon her because she was not married and had a child that clearly did not look like her. By the time I had made it to high school, I decided on my own to leave Christianity.

It was in college that I learned about Paganism in the courses I was taking. I realized Paganism was something I really felt drawn to and told my mother I wanted to look into it -- she told me she was, too, and probably always had been a Pagan.

We didn't really tell many people because we did not know anything really about Paganism yet. We knew what it wasn't -- and that's what appealed to us. So we decided to do two things: read and join the local Pagan group. We tried being part of a group with moderate success. I was used to being the only person of color in a group but I felt really out of place and not really welcomed. I realized later it wasn't because of the color of my skin, it was just jitters from meeting new people.

My mother and I started with Scott Cunningham's *Wicca: A Guide for the Solitary Practitioner*, and she decided she was going to focus mostly on Herbalism. However, I took a bit longer deciding on my interest.

I jumped into doing spells without realizing what I was doing. Consequently, the spells either didn't work or backfired in my face. So I decided to do some more research. My mother bought me a book called, *Illustrated Dictionary of Mythology*. I glanced through it and saw the Chinese Gods section; I read a little bit about Kuan Yin and became more interested in her.

Kuan Yin is the Buddhist goddess of mercy. Her popularity spread to China from India, where she is worshiped to help the childless and those who want to conceive. She helps those who are sick, is the patron of travelers and farmers, and protects souls in the underworld. I found Kuan Yin interesting because she was the epitome of compassion and mercy. I prayed to her a lot for compassion.

In group discussions with Pagans about the Goddess I would explain I liked having a patron goddess. I would tell them it was Kuan Yin and they looked at me weird. It wasn't something a "Black" person would do. It irritated me because I do not like being put in a box. I don't think people meant to be rude at all. I tried not to let this bother me, but it just didn't work.

I began a new interest in the Ancient Greeks and Romans during my college years, and fell in love with the Olympians. I felt a real kinship with Athena. She is a strong character -- very smart and bright. She is kind of angry, and I totally understood that aspect of her. Athena is the goddess of war and crafts. I liked that she is contrary like that.

I liked that she is a smart, crafty woman who is very much active in the affairs of humanity. She doesn't just sit back and allow things to happen.

As I learned more about Athena, the more I loved her. I, like Athena, enjoyed just being a woman. I have been rejected so many times from society because I was too black or not black enough or too fat. I was too polar opposite for people. Athena helped me get through that phase because she is not who she appears to be either.

My energies were bouncing everywhere and I was trying so hard to prove I wasn't the "typical black person." I just did not want to be stereotyped. When I told people I was Pagan the immediate question was "Voodoo"? I struggled within myself to steer clear from anything from the African continent because it was really irritating that people expected that of my practice.

I continued to struggle with my beliefs. At this point I didn't even really KNOW what I wanted. I knew I was gearing toward "Goddess Worship" but what did that really mean?

I reread *Wicca: A Guide for the Solitary Practitioner* and I finally understood what the Goddess meant to me. She is a loving mother; fertility, growth, wisdom and caring. She is stern yet tender; She encompasses what being a mother is supposed to be. MY mother was those things and every time I think of my mother I think of the Goddess.

My mother's health started to decline to the point where she needed oxygen all the time and full-time care. I knew Athena had gotten me through some tough times but I needed to move into a new stage. I imagine as most people get chronologically older they get wiser (I hope they do). I was one of those that needed a good swift kick in the butt as well as getting tripped (figuratively) in order to learn.

I was never one to "get it" the first time, but when my mom nearly died a couple of years ago I finally got a little wiser. She was almost taken from me, and that moment I realized I could no longer hold onto the fact that no matter what I try to present myself as, people are going to see me as they see me: a Black person. I couldn't change THEIR image of me but I could change my attitude about

it.
    I realized that I needed to make a clear choice of what path I wanted to follow. My energies were chaotic and my "self" was all over the place. I was so caught up in what I didn't want that I had put up a wall. The journey to get to this point was long and hard. Luckily my mother recovered and I got several more years with her. I realized I was really interested in the Avalonian/Celtic/Faery religion the entire time. It's a little bit of everything that I am.
    My mother also liked faery magick and we have many faeries. My mother's faery is a little pink faery and she saw a little pink ball bounce around our home. The one attached to me is a brownie that enjoyed misplacing my keys. He's green because sometimes I see a green ball of energy flitting around.
    My mother lost her battle with lung problems and passed away March of 2013. As I grapple with her death, my faith has become even more of a focus to me. I knew at that moment that the Avalonian Tradition was something I wanted. I have a book called *Avalon Within: A Sacred Journey of Myth, Mystery and Inner Wisdom*. The one quote I absolutely love from this book is:
    "Women of Avalon embrace the female energetic power -- the inward turning spiral that leads to the sacred, sovereign, fully actualized center within us all. It is a path that reclaims inner darkness and births the inner priestess into being -- transforming fear into love, and pain into power."
    My mother got this book for me for Yule and I didn't really look at it until after she had passed away. My journey to Avalon as a person of color has been interesting. I have always found the Arthurian Myth interesting and fascinating but I was too scared to enjoy it because I was not White. I realized before it was too late that it is ok, it may not be traditionally what people think I'm supposed

to do, but I like breaking down barriers. My mother always taught me to walk my own path.

I am, however, only at the beginning of this journey -- learning to be aware as a woman, not just a woman of color. I don't suspect it will be easy, but that's ok. For this journey I have found Brigit. I remember praying to Brigit and asking her to make sure my mom got to the Isle of Avalon safely. I could not bear the thought of my mom lost somewhere. I don't know why I called for Brigit but it seemed like the right thing to do.

I decided it might be a good idea to read a little more about Brigit and found out she is a goddess of many things including healing, and fertility. She is sometimes considered a three-fold goddess of healing; smithing and forging -- of finding inspiration. For me Brigit is her healing aspect; I have also found kinship in her because she is many things to many people.

Now writing this I realize I can follow any path I want and what is right for me isn't right for everyone. It's been hard because I think in society we pigeonhole people to make ourselves feel better. Everything has a place and a name; if it's out of place we completely freak out. I don't mind breaking-down barriers and making people slightly uncomfortable. I am what I am and I am ok with this.

Bibliography

Cunningham, Scott. *Wicca: For the Solitary Practitioner*. St. Paul: Llewellyn Publications, 1996.

Cotterell, Arthur. *The Encyclopedia of Mythology*. New York: Anness Publishing Limited, 1996.

Telyndru, Jhenah. *Avalon Within: A Sacred Journey of Myth, Mystery, and Inner Wisdom*. Woodbury, 2005

Wilkinson, Philip. *Illustrated Dictionary of Mythology: Heroes, heroines, Gods and Goddesses from*

Around the World. England: DK Publishing, 1998.
"Brigid." Encyclopedia Mythica. 2013. Encyclopedia Mythica Online. 30 Jul. 2013 <http://www.pantheon.org/articles/b/brigid.html>

Biographies

Nadirah Adeye, MA (aka *The Sacred Sensualist*), is a priestess, mother, writer, lover and public ritualist and is the creator of Sacred Sensual Living. She lives and works in the San Francisco Bay Area, and is committed to supporting women in living lives of peace, pleasure, authenticity and fulfillment. She adores the book *The Kin of Ata are Waiting for You*, and strives to live each day, like the kin, in service of the dream. She is also pretty sure that, since this writing thing is going to continue, she probably needs to write a standard bio and make use of it in times like these. Her web site is www.nadirahadeye.com

Clio Ajana is a queer third degree High Priestess, Hellenic Alexandrian Tradition and Education Coordinator for Our Lady of Celestial Fire, EOCTO. A native Marylander and Minnesota transplant, she is deeply passionate about numerology, astrology, and writing as a spiritual practice. A writer for Daughters of Eve, her writing interests include how race, homophobia and religious non-acceptance intersect, how Paganism can address the needs of aging Pagans or non-Pagan relatives, and rituals for self and group empowerment. She can be found on Facebook as Clio Ajana and on her blog www.clioajana.com.

Crystal Blanton is a High Priestess, counselor/social worker, graduate student in a Social Work program at a California State University and a published author. She is the author of two books, Pain and Faith in a Wiccan World, Bridging the Gap: Working within the Dynamics of Pagan Groups and Society, and is the editor of Shades of Faith: Minority Voices in Paganism. She writes for the Patheos blog "Daughters of Eve," and is a columnist for Sage

Woman Magazine and The Wild Hunt. She currently works with disenfranchised youth in West Oakland doing social work and clinical services, and researches and writes about the impact of systemic failure and social injustice on people of color.

Flame Bridhesdottir is the nom de plume of a middle aged Pagan woman of no particular import. She carries a miniature Dr. Who in her pocket at all times, to remind herself to be her own hero. When not mothering or wifeing, she can be found reading the entire internet and dreaming wistfully of moving to the United Kingdom. She makes a mean pot of soup and refers to herself as The Soup Witch. Her favorite person is a cat named Zelda. Zelda's favorite person is herself as well, but she allows Flame to tag along. Flame really loves being a witch, and can't believe she ever lived any other way. She can be found on Facebook as flame.bridhesdottir or sporadically on her blog at thiswitchswork.blogspot.com

Leslie Brooks lives in Southeast Ohio. She lives with her lovely three-legged cat named Ozzy. She graduated from Ohio University with a degree in Classical History, and enjoys being with family and friends. She enjoys reading about Avalon and Faery Magick

Janet Callahan is a priestess, wife, and mother of two complicated former preemies living near Detroit. She has a day job as an engineer, but has finally decided that she wants to be a writer and artist when she grows up. You can find all of her projects at
http://www.janetcallahan.com

Alexandra Chauran is a second-generation fortuneteller, a third degree elder High Priestess of British Traditional Wicca, and the Queen of a coven. As a professional psychic intuitive for over a decade, she serves thousands of clients in the Seattle area and globally through her website. She is certified in tarot and has been interviewed on National Public Radio and other major media outlets. Alexandra is currently pursuing a doctoral degree, lives in Issaquah, Washington and can be found online at EarthShod.com

Yutaka Furuki has drawn to the Western traditions for many years. He is practicing the Runes and the Northern Tradition and doing his own experiments with Magic in a personalized style.

Abel R. Gomez a queer Latino writer, scholar and activist dedicated to collective empowerment and transformational ceremony. An initiate of Hindu Shakta Tantra, he is also a priest in the Reclaiming Tradition. He has facilitated workshops at universities and within his community on earth-based spirituality, ritual, and the magical arts. Abel is currently pursuing an MA in Religious Studies with an emphasis on religions of Indigenous peoples.

Olivia Haynes writes Black Witch, a blog centered on the intersection of being Black and Pagan. She also currently resides in her hometown of Baltimore City, MD.

Yvonne Esther Nieves lives and works in Chicago as a certified Reiki Master Teacher (RMT) at Urban Escape Healing Studio, is trained in crystal healing therapy, and is a member of the World Metaphysical Association. She holds a Bachelors of Arts Degree in Anthropology from Northeastern Illinois University and is currently studying New Orleans rootwork and conjure at Crossroads University. She is initiated as an apetebi in the Ifa religion.

Luna Pantera is a native San Franciscan and mother of an amazing 24 year old. Luna is a Daughter of: Oshun, Brigit, Isis and so many other Goddesses that have claimed her over the years. She is an out of the Broom Closet Witch, professional tarot reader, Navigator at the Cross Roads, Master Reiki Practitioner, and body worker specializing on adult survivors of sexual assault. She currently works at the Mystic Dream in Walnut Creek, CA. She is the founder of Theatre of the Ancestors. She is a feature author in the anthology, "Shades of Faith; Minority Voices in Paganism," and is currently working on her forthcoming trilogy, "Both Sides Now." She co-facilitates retreats up to Mount Shasta. You can find out more about Luna's services at Lunastouch.com.

Dr. Katharyn Privett-Duren (Seba O'Kiley) is Beloved Woman of the Gangani Tribe of Alabama, a family tradition that marries the practices and theologies of both the Eastern Band of Cherokee and ancient Central Ireland Celts. Seba holds a doctorate in Philosophy and has taught in the university setting for almost fourteen years. The Gangani Tribe was restructured in 2009 to include oath-bound (but not necessarily blood-related) tribal members in an effort to preserve its lineage. The Tribe focuses heavily on the sacredness of the Earth, the cycles of Her seasons and the importance of returning to a tribal/sustainable structure in the South. As such, Gangani members are part of a family; membership is carefully considered for at least one year (including auditing time) and subject to Tribal vote. The Tribe is specifically invested in the continued education and healthy nurturance of our magical children living within the Bible Belt.

In addition to her spiritual work, Seba is an avid gardener, a wife, a mother of four souls and is expecting her first tribal grandchild this fall. Her essay, "The Other Southerner," represents the very first public outing of her work under her government name. Seba/Kat continues to strive towards inclusion and acceptance for all Witches and Pagans within the Deep South. As a "baby Crone," she has fully entered the public sphere at a time in her life that

insists upon an ethos of wisdom, teaching and servitude to the land that has sustained her magic for nearly half a century. You may follow her blog at:
Southernkitchenwitch.com.

Nathaniel Puckett is a Pagan veteran from Buford, Georgia, where he lives with his family coven and is a member of Willow Dragonstone Community. Find him on Face Book at
https://www.facebook.com/puckettnathaniellee.

Rt. Rev. Anniitra Ravenmoon is an ArchPriestess with the Fellowship of Isis, worldwide. She is Founder of Temple of Isis, Long Beach, Ca., and Lycem of The Nubian Moon, which hosts, Book Salons, Rituals, and Spiritual gatherings. She is founder of "Circle of The Sacred Cauldron, which celebrates Full, and Dark Moon rituals and ceremonies. She is Also ~~Priest & Personal Assistant to MaShiAat Oloya, Kindred Of ShiEndra, and a Certified Level II HaVla Instructor, Ordained High Priestess ; in the Dianic tradition.. She designs Silver goddess themed jewelry, and beads Shamanic Necklaces. Rev. Ravenmoon, also teaches North African style dance (belly dance) and Ritual Sacred Dance.

Sandra Santiago is a Chicago-based early childhood educator, activist, published artist/illustrator, artisan, performance poet and actress. She has a BA in education from Roosevelt University, Chicago, Illinois. Her first book of poetry is *The Rhythm of Everyday Things* (2014). She has previously had her poetry published in several anthologies including *Cantologia* (2013), *Rebeldes: A Proyecto Latina Anthology* (2013), *The Poetically Unspoken Anthology* (2010), and *Shades of Faith; Minority Voices in Paganism* (2011). She is creator and curator of the Butterfly Poetry Project, a venue where women are valued as human beings growing, working and living in a state of neutrality and peace. She is initiated into Ifa, Palo Mayombe, practices Espiritismo (Spiritism), and is also a Reiki practitioner.

Szmeralda Shanel MA is a visual, ritual and performance artist. She is an initiate in the Anderson Feri/Faery tradition, a founding member of CAYA coven and an ordained priestess of Isis/Auset with the Fellowship of Isis and the Temple of Isis. Szmeralda is the founder of The Iseum of Black Isis, an iseum dedicated to Goddess Spirituality and Sacred Arts. She currently lives in Chicago, IL and works as a teaching artist, expressive arts therapist/facilitator, and tarot reader.
www.blackisismagic.com

Rose Skye: Like many artistic children, Rose was told not to be an artist because artists don't make any money. So instead of being an artist she decided - like a proper Pollyanna - to be a writer instead. Apparently, it's more respectable to be a starving writer than a starving artist, and she had to do a lot of jobs in between writing before she was able to turn it into a living. She is a hereditary mystic and has walked the Crooked Path for over 30 years, taking various branches, twists and turns upon the way. Some of those winding ways were so odd people have encouraged her to write a biography, but she still refuses to do it as no one would believe it anyway. She therefore writes fiction and paints, as fantasy and fiction is easier to believe and admire for many people.

Jayde Van Ter Pool (Lakitsym), born and raised in London, England, now living in the United States with her family. She is a practicing solitary Witch, with lineage in African and European Witchcraft. She is also an accomplished Children's Book Illustrator, poet and Vocalist.

Pablo M.A Vazquez III considers himself many things,

including performer, poet, eternal student, sometimes scholar, agitator, bard-magus, and all the other titles that float in his imagination. Of Afro-Latin-Irish-Basque stock, his family has constantly found itself in mystical and revolutionary camps, which reflects his upbringing and the shaping of just the sort of person he is today. A true lover of Freedom and Passion, he champions love and unity, liberty and danger, creativity and aesthetics, as a student of the great esotericists of old and the great radical theorists of new. Born alongside the Canal in the Republic of Panama, he strangely does not like extreme heat and views his perfect weather to be something akin to Fimbulwinter, but he definitely is a child of the Caribbean, with all of its mystic glory, tropical paradises and delicious culinary trappings. Pablo spends his time traversing various underground and subcultural communities, ranging from Science-Fiction and Fantasy fandom to Underground Rap to radical bookstores to, of course, magical lodges and mystic circles. He hopes his poetry can spark a revolution of the soul and create a Palace of Liberty in your heart, where you'll be free to wander and become truly infinite.

Heaven Walker is a High Priestess, Scholar, Teacher, Writer, and a member of the American Academy of Religion. Her publications include "Invoking the Queen" in Shades of Faith: Minority Voices in Paganism and "Our Family Coalition" in The 21st Century Motherhood Movement: Mothers Speak Out on Why We Need to Change the World and How to Do It. Heaven Walker is an Elder and co-founder of the Come As You Are Coven, and the founder of the Grove of Artemis women's moon circle. She is also a legally ordained interfaith minister who offers professional tarot card readings, spiritual counseling, wedding ceremonies, and rites of passage. However, Heaven considers her most sacred work to be motherhood and is the former leader of the "Sprouts" pagan parenting and ritual group. She hopes to eventually create an earth based spirituality centered children's scouting troop.

Cecily Joy Willowe, M.Div is a radical, eclectic, solitary Wiccan of over 10 years. She holds a Master of Divinity degree from Naropa University in Boulder, CO. After receiving her degree, she has gone on to work at local homeless shelters. She is passionate about Contemporary Paganism, African Diasporic spirituality, Spirit Guide communication, meditation and tarot. She is always looking for new interfaith approaches to victim advocacy, diversity work and other forms of social justice. You can find Cecily blogging over at her microblog: virtualchaplain.tumblr.com.

Alisa Kuumba Zuwena: Like most of us, Alisa Kuumba Zuwena was born with a gift. Her gift, however, is unique because she is able to communicate and hear messages from loved ones who have crossed over and passed on. As a young child, she realized this ability and has been using it to help others for over 40 years now. If you have heard of John Edwards or Sylvia Brown, Kuumba Zuwena is very similar in her approach. She has traveled to West Africa, The Bahamas and nationally as an Intuitive Artist/Workshop Spiritual Facilitator. Alisa is the proud mother of four, residing in Asheville, NC.

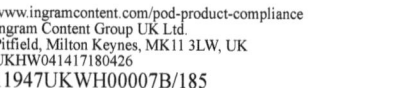